CANADIAN CONCEPTS

CONCEPTS

Second Edition

6

Lynda Berish
Sandra Thibaudeau

Collège Marie-Victorin

Prentice Hall Allyn and Bacon Canada
Scarborough, Ontario

Canadian Cataloguing in Publication Data

Berish, Lynda, date
  Canadian concepts 6

2nd ed.
ISBN 0-13-591736-0

1. English language—Textbooks for second language learners.*
2. English Language—Grammar.   3. English language—Problems,
exercises, etc.   I. Thibaudeau, Sandra, date.   II. Title.

PE1128.B476 1997   428.2'4   C96-931831-6

© Copyright 1998 Prentice-Hall Canada Inc.,
    Scarborough, Ontario
A Division of Simon & Schuster/A Viacom Company

Allyn and Bacon, Inc., Needham Heights, Massachusetts
Prentice-Hall, Inc., Upper Saddle River, New Jersey
Prentice-Hall International (UK) Limited, London
Prentice-Hall of Australia, Pty., Ltd., Sydney
Prentice-Hall Hispanoamericana, S. A., Mexico
Prentice-Hall of India Private Limited, New Delhi
Prentice-Hall of Japan, Inc., Tokyo
Prentice-Hall of Southeast Asia (PTE) Ltd., Singapore
Simon & Schuster Asia Private Limited, Singapore
Editora Prentice-Hall do Brasil Ltda., Rio de Janeiro

ISBN 0-13-591736-0

Acquisitions editor: Dominique Roberge
Developmental editor: Marta Tomins
Production editor: Elynor Kagan
Editorial assistant: Rita Self
Production coordinator: Sharon Houston
Design: Monica Kompter
Layout: Joseph Chin
Text illustrations: Paul McCusker
Unit opening illlustrations: Carole Giguère
Cover image: Steve Short/First Light, Mauve Sky, Ogilvie

Printed and bound in Canada

1 2 3 4 5   99 98 97

Visit the Prentice Hall Canada web site! Send us
your comments, browse our catalogues, and more.
www.phcanada.com Or reach us through e-mail at
phabinfo_pubcanada@prenhall.com

Credits

The authors would like to acknowledge, with thanks, the
organizations, publications, and individuals who gave
permission to reprint articles used in this text.

Unit 1: "World Wide Web: 3 English Words" by Michael
Spector reprinted by permission of *The New York Times*.

Unit 2: "Ice Dream" by Richard Lapalme reprinted by
permission of the author.

Unit 3: "Price of gold too high" by Bill Benner reprinted
by permission of Associated Press.

Unit 4: "Justice Without Courtrooms" by Debbie Parkes
reprinted by permission of the author and *The Gazette*
(Montreal).

Unit 5: "Do tobacco ads work on teens?" by Sarah Scott
reprinted by permission of *The Gazette* (Montreal).

Unit 6: "Cancer-society endorsement of products under
attack" by Steve Sakson reprinted by permission of
Associated Press.

Unit 7: "The All-American Fire Trap" by Jon McMillan
reprinted by permission of *The New York Times*.

Unit 8: "Genetic Job Loss" by Velida Starcevich reprinted
by permission of *The Observer*.

Unit 9: "Is tabloid TV getting out of hand?" by Ted Shaw
reprinted by permission of the author and *The Windsor
Star*.

Unit 10: From *Emotional Intelligence* by Daniel Goleman.
Copyright © 1995 by Daniel Goleman. Used by permission
of Bantam Books, a division of Bantam Doubleday Dell
Publishing Group, Inc.

This book is dedicated to Jenny (Cherna) Goldman, now 97 years old, who always encouraged further education and achievement.

We would like to express our appreciation to Millicent and Max Goldman for their proofreading, and to Tara Berish for transcribing the tapes.

CONTENTS

LISTENING ACTIVITIES	VIDEO ACTIVITIES
1. Cyberzone	
	1. Yaohan Market (6:08 minutes)
2. Silken Laumann's Gold Medal	
	2. Alternative Punishment (23:47 minutes)
3. Tobacco Companies Under Attack	
	3. Corporate Donations (5:10 minutes)

LISTENING ACTIVITIES	VIDEO ACTIVITIES
4. Taking the Case	
	4. Your Genetic Profile (13:54 minutes)
	5. Drug Alert (8:52 minutes)
5. Doing What You Love	

TO THE TEACHER

The *Canadian Concepts* Series

The new edition of the popular *Canadian Concepts* series retains the Canadian focus designed to help students feel at home and integrate into the community. In the new edition, exercises and activities have been graded and refocussed to provide a careful build-up of skills throughout the series. *Canadian Concepts 1* is paced to accommodate the needs of post-literacy students. *Canadian Concepts 2* provides a controlled expansion of survival English topics, vocabulary, and structure. *Canadian Concepts 3* and *4* provide the concrete themes necessary to reinforce language while offering a greater challenge in terms of pacing, tasks, and input. CBC video clips are integrated into the units in *Canadian Concepts 4, 5,* and *6.*

The *Canadian Concepts* series uses a communicative approach. The method offers productive strategies for language learning based on student-centred interaction. Many new activities, games, and opportunities for speaking have been incorporated into the series to encourage maximum student participation in classroom activities. The pedagogical model presents students with challenging listening or reading input, leading them through pre-activities and strategies that make the input comprehensible. In addition to these fluency-building activities, dictation, grammar and spelling, and vocabulary work focus on improving students' accuracy.

Canadian Concepts 6

Canadian Concepts 6 expands on the more controversial, opinion-based themes and activities introduced in *Canadian Concepts 5.* As in *Canadian Concepts 5,* students are challenged to deal with more abstract, thought-provoking material. Topics for debate are outlined at the end of the book to provide practice in sophisticated oral expression after each unit. Throughout the book, stimulating themes and a wide variety of activities keep students interested and involved.

Canadian Concepts 6 is made up of ten self-contained units. Core activities focus on authentic reading from a variety of newspapers and magazines, and listening and video materials from the CBC. Video clips have been selected from CBC news programs such as *Market Place, Venture,* and *Country Canada.* Grammar and writing activities provide ample opportunity for practice and expression.

Throughout the units, students are asked to work on challenging materials that focus on social and cultural issues. Each unit begins and ends with an activity entitled "What's Your Take On This?", which encourages students to develop a personal stake as they voice their opinions and questions on the theme of the unit. A "Perfect Your English" feature takes a fun approach to exploring some of the idiosyncrasies of English, including figurative language, metaphors, and oxymorons.

Teachers and students will appreciate the simple format and lively appearance of the materials, with attractive illustrations that support the themes. They will also enjoy browsing through the Canadian Capsules that provide valuable background information on Canada.

KEY TO SYMBOLS

 Work with a partner

 Listening activity

 Work in a group

 Video activity

 Writing activity

 Discussion activity

 Reading activity

Teacher's Manual and Resource Package

A comprehensive Teacher's Manual and Resource Package provides a wide scope of activities for building academic and professional skills, including skills needed for various types of writing, note-taking, and oral reporting. It also includes an answer key and tape scripts.

THREE ENGLISH WORDS

GETTING TO KNOW YOU

Work in a group. Discuss these questions.

1. At what age did you begin to learn English?

2. Whose idea was it for you to learn English (your parents', the school system's, your friends', your own)?

3. Would you say that English is an easy language to learn? Explain.

4. What are some reasons you are happy to speak English well?

5. How many people speak your native language?

6. Where do people speak your native language besides in your country?

7. How many languages do you speak?

8. In what circumstances do you use these languages?

9. For which activities do you use English?

WHAT'S YOUR TAKE ON THIS?

International Communication

Before you go any further in the unit, work in a group to discuss these questions.

1. What **four** languages are the most widely spoken in the world?

2. What reasons could people have for **not** wanting to speak English? (political, sociological, etc.)

3. What are some things a person in modern times would find it difficult to do without a good knowledge of English?

4. Who do you think uses the Internet most, and for what?

5. Have you used the Internet?

6. Who controls the Internet?

7. Do you think that the kind of international communication made possible by modern technology is having a positive impact on the world?

LINGUA FRANCA

A   Read the paragraph quickly. Then listen and write while your teacher dictates.

There are over 200 major languages spoken in the world today, but some languages are more widely used than others. Over the centuries, four languages have emerged as the most used. They are now spoken or understood by about half the world's population. In order of number of speakers, these languages are Mandarin Chinese, English, Arabic, and Spanish. The fastest growing *lingua franca*, however, is English. It has become the language of diplomacy, airline communications, science, and the computer industry. English has become an international language, shared by many people whose native languages are different.

CANADIAN CAPSULES

A *lingua franca* is a language adopted as a common means of communication between people who speak different native tongues. There are now more people in the world who speak English as a second language than there are people who speak it as their native tongue.

B Look at the statement below and decide which of the sentences support it.

> English is a **strange** choice as a *lingua franca*.

1. English is spoken in many geographical areas of the world.

2. There are many idiomatic expressions in English.

3. English is useful when you travel outside your country.

4. Spelling in English is not logical, as it is in Italian.

5. Unlike French and Japanese, English uses a complex system of stress and intonation.

6. The Korean alphabet is much easier than the English one.

7. Most people who have to learn English don't really want to.

8. Thai and Russian scientists usually communicate in English.

WORLD WIDE WEB: THREE ENGLISH WORDS

  A Scan the article to find the following information:

1. the three English words referred to in the title

2. reasons why the Internet is seen by some as a great **democratic** influence

3. a sign of the popularity of the Internet among adult Americans

4. changes the Internet has brought to people overseas in the last ten years

5. three examples of people using the Internet, as cited in paragraph 4

6. three reasons English became the common language of the Internet

7. Antoly Voronov's feelings about the Internet

8. the group to which the majority of English speakers today belong

9. why Japan is less bothered than other countries by the hegemony of English on the Internet

10. why the Internet can be considered beneficial to "have nots"

CANADIAN CAPSULES

Unlike the United States, which does not have an official language, Canada has two official languages: English and French.

World Wide Web: Three English Words

Michael Spector

1. The Internet has been pretty universally viewed as one of the great democratic advances of the late twentieth century. Nothing in human history has ever made more information more readily available to more people at lower cost.

2. Perhaps only the car and the television have had a more immediate impact on the habits of twentieth-century Americans. According to a recent Nielsen study, adults in the United States spend more time collectively browsing the Internet every week than they do watching video cassettes. Nearly 20 million American adults say they use the World Wide Web regularly and as many as 2 million have bought goods and services on the Web.

Yo, Cairo!

3. The impact overseas has been at least as dramatic. If you live in Cairo, Jakarta, or St. Petersburg, you can now exchange information with people from Athens, Lima, or Lake Louise. For many, educational opportunities that could not even be imagined ten years ago are only a few key strokes away. To study molecular genetics, all you need to get into Harvard University Library or the medical library at Sweden's Karolinska Institute, is a phone line and a computer.

4. And, it turns out, a solid command of the English language. Because whether you are a French intellectual pursuing the cutting edge of international film theory, a Japanese paleobotanist curious about a newly discovered set of primordial fossils, or an American teenager concerned about Magic Johnson's jump shot, the Internet and the World Wide Web really only work as great unifiers if you speak English.

5. Mostly that's by accident. The Internet started in the United States and the computer hackers whose reality has always been virtual are almost all American. By the time the net spread, its linguistic patterns—like its principal architecture and best software—were all made in the USA. That's not surprising since English has become the international language of commerce and communication—and since educated foreigners are far more likely to learn a second language than are any class of Americans. But increasingly that language must be English.

"Colonialism!"

6. "It is just incredible when I hear people talking about how open the web is," said Antoly Voronov, the director of Glasnet, Russia's best-known Internet provider. "It is the ultimate act of intellectual colonialism. The product comes from America so we must either adapt to English or stop using it. That is the right of any business. But if you are talking about a technology that is supposed to open the world to hundreds of millions of people, you are joking. This just makes the world into new sorts of 'haves' and 'have nots.'"

7. There are, of course, plenty of Web pages in Russian, Japanese, French, German and Chinese. It is possible for anybody in almost any country to carry on an electronic relationship with other people who speak his or her language. And eventually computers may help translate a search from one language to another.

8. But for now, if you want to take full advantage of the Internet, there is only really one way to do it: learn English, which has more than ever become America's greatest export. It has been estimated that there are now more people who speak English as a foreign language than as their first language. English is already the language of diplomacy, scientific discourse, air traffic control. But the implications of turning an international computer network into another platform for English—and the values it represents—are immense.

9. According to Christian Huitema, who is on the board of the Internet Society which tries to set world standards, it takes about 2 million potential customers to establish a workable market. Japan now has close to 3 million, and it has become far less dependent on and bothered by the hegemony of English than other countries. "As the Internet grows, the body of people speaking languages other than English will grow as well," says Mr. Huitema.

10. "The effect of the Internet is to make information available at minimum cost and effort," he said. "This is most beneficial to the current 'have nots' of our societies. High-school students in desolated urban areas or university students in Africa can gain information on the Internet that is currently available only in libraries of educated parents or Ivy League Universities. Learning basic English in order to reap that benefit seems like a sensible investment."

  B Use vocabulary from the text to complete this puzzle.

Across

3. presently (paragraph 10)
4. scanning (paragraph 2)
7. huge (paragraph 8)
8. connectors (paragraph 4)
9. main (paragraph 5)
12. conversation (paragraph 8)
13. harvest (paragraph 10)

Down

1. adjust (paragraph 6)
2. control (paragraph 9)
5. abroad (paragraph 3)
6. barren (paragraph 10)
9. seeking (paragraph 4)
10. lots (paragraph 7)
11. understanding (paragraph 4)

LANGUAGE AND CULTURE

Work in a group. Discuss the questions.

1. Does the second sentence of the article remind you of a famous statement by Winston Churchill? Explain.

2. What is a Nielsen study?

3. In which countries are the following: Cairo, Jakarta, St. Petersburg, Lima, Athens, and Lake Louise?

4. With which sport is a "jump shot" associated?

5. Explain the following phrase from paragraph 5: "computer hackers whose reality has always been virtual."

6. What are "haves" and "have nots"?

7. What is an Ivy League university?

Present Perfect

The present perfect aspect is used for an action or state that began in the past and continues in the present.

> The impact of the Internet **has been** dramatic. (and it continues to be)

The present perfect is also used for an action or state that occurred at some unspecified time in the past and continues to have some relationship to the present.

To form the present perfect, use the auxiliary verb **have** (**has**) + the past participle of the main verb. Regular past participles are the same as the simple past tense form. Irregular past participles have to be learned by heart. (See the Appendix of irregular verbs on page 132.)

    A   Work in pairs to complete the chart.

be (am, is, are)	was/were	_____
became	become	_____
begin	began	_____
blow	blew	_____
break	broke	_____
bring	brought	_____
choose	chose	_____

➡

come	came	_____
do	did	_____
drink	drank	_____
drive	drove	_____
eat	ate	_____
forget	forgot	_____
get	got	_____
give	gave	_____
go	went	_____
know	knew	_____
run	ran	_____
see	saw	_____
shake	shook	_____
show	showed	_____
take	took	_____
throw	threw	_____
wear	wore	_____
write	wrote	_____

B   Complete the sentences with the correct form of the present perfect.

apply exist become see dream be work use make speak

1. Nothing _____ ever _____ more information available to more people at lower cost.

2. The impact of the Web overseas _____ at least as dramatic.

3. Much of the best software is made in English since English _____ the international language of communication.

4. How long _____ the technology needed for the Internet _____?

5. People over 30 _____ many amazing technological advances in their lifetimes.

6. Hiroshi lived in the United States as a child and he _____ English all his life.

7. The computer sales representative _____ for the same company for many years.

8. How many people here _____ the World Wide Web to get information they needed?

9. Fred _____ to many companies since he graduated in the spring.

10. My friends _____ of owning a computer since they visited the technology fair.

C Choose the simple past or present perfect form of the verbs.

1. Yesterday someone _____ (forget) to turn off the computer before leaving the office.

2. Po Yee _____ (know) word processing ever since she graduated from secretarial college.

3. I'm sorry but I _____ (not/have) a chance to reply to your message since I got back.

4. Karen _____ (visit) the computer exhibit when she was at the trade fair last week.

5. When the first computer was invented, nobody _____ (imagine) that it would have such an impact.

6. Annabel _____ (speak) French for as long as I can remember.

7. Two years ago I _____ (get) my first big break when I was hired as a computer programmer.

8. When Richard was in Japan, he _____ (teach) English to students in a high school in Kyoto.

9. The Internet _____ (become) a fact of life in most university libraries in North American.

10. The World Wide Web _____ (have) an enormous impact on how information is transmitted.

CANADIAN CAPSULES

English, like many other languages, is influenced by many different cultures. In Canada some words, including "moose" and "canoe," have come from the languages of Aboriginal peoples.

WRITE ABOUT IT

The Language of Shakespeare

In the past century, English has increased its importance as an international *lingua franca*. Choose one topic and write about it.

a) The Role of English in the World Today

   or

b) The Impact of the Internet

CYBERZONE

 CBC

LISTENING ACTIVITY **1**

 A Discuss the following questions.

1. Have you used the Internet?

2. If so, for what purpose?

3. Why do you think people are so fascinated by the Internet?

4. Where can you get access to the Internet if you do not have a computer that is linked to it?

 B Listen to the short news item. Then work in pairs and tell each other everything you remember.

PERFECT YOUR ENGLISH

Bridging the Gap

How do you fill the silence when you aren't quite sure what you want to say next?

Well, you could use "well" to start your sentence—as we did here. Fillers and bridges are sounds or meaningless little phrases that many of us use as we search for words or collect our thoughts. Some common fillers are "um," "er," "well," "anyway," "like," and "you know."

Researchers have found that some people use "um" as many as 10 or 15 times a minute, and as many as 1000 times an hour! In fact, most of us don't realize we are using these vocal pauses. One reason we use them is to signal that we intend to continue speaking.

Fillers exist in all languages, of course. A common Russian filler is "znachit" which translates as "it means." Spanish speakers often use "este" as a bridge. It translates literally as "this." Germans say "oder" or "nicht" to fill conversational space. The British have the strange custom of making a "listening noise" by drawing out the sound "mmmmmmm."

The Japanese use the word "nah" as a pause in the conversation and they often signal attention with "hai." This word translates literally as "yes" although it doesn't mean "yes," but rather "I hear you." Indonesians use "unh, unh" to show interest—a little confusing for Canadians who use "unh, unh" to mean "no."

Discuss the questions.

1. What are some bridges your teacher or classmates use?

2. Which words do you hear used as fillers in news broadcasts?

3. What are some fillers that are commonly used in your language?

4. What do these expressions mean literally?

5. Which bridges or fillers do you commonly use yourself in English?

AT LAST

Now that you have finished the unit, go back to the activity "What's Your Take On This?" and discuss the questions again.

UNIT 2

BEING CANADIAN: SLICES OF LIFE

WHAT'S YOUR TAKE ON THIS?

It Isn't Always Winter

Canada has been described as "a few acres of snow." While snow is certainly part of the experience of living in Canada, it doesn't tell the whole story. Perhaps that is why the weather is one of the most common topics of conversation amongst Canadians.

Discuss these questions in a group.

1. How much impact do geography and climate have on people's ideas and lifestyles?

2. To what extent does cold weather affect the average Canadian?

3. How do people describe their experiences and preparations in coping with winter in Canada?

4. How might children's experiences of winter be different from those of adults?

5. How do the changing seasons affect people in Canada?

11

ICE DREAM

A   Read the article and then, in a group, discuss the questions that follow.

Ice Dream

Richard Lapalme

1.   When I was a boy, it seemed that there was always a reason for a party in my family. The Christmas holidays had barely passed when we'd all gather for my grandfather's birthday in early January. Later in January, my parents had their birthdays and then came my grandmother's birthday in February. There was always a big event and the family celebrated it on the Saturday closest to the date. Back in 1961, when I was 10, Nanny's birthday celebration fell on Saturday, February 28.

2.   I loved these parties because I'd get to see all my uncles, aunts, and cousins. Sometimes distant relatives, some I'd only heard about, dropped by to extend their wishes. The house was a bazaar of pleasant sounds and aromas. My aunt Dora, always dancing, tried to teach us the tango or cha-cha. Mostly we just spun around and stepped on her toes.

3.   I remember that it began to rain as we arrived. My dad asked my grandmother for some cardboard because the rain was already freezing to the car windows. I watched from the living-room window as Dad secured the cardboard, cut from a grocery box, to the windshield with the wipers. My uncle Mario told us why Dad was putting the cardboard on, as he and the other men scrambled to find more cardboard to protect their windshields. That was fine, I thought, but what about the other windows?

4.   I have forgotten the details of the party; however, I do remember sitting in the car, side windows thick with ice, watching Dad peel the cardboard from the windshield. It actually worked; the cardboard had protected the windshield and it was ice-free. A few peep holes were opened up in the other windows by the joint forces of the car heater and Dad's methodical scraping. On the drive home, the rhythmic flowing and ebbing of Dad's reflected shadow on the back seat lulled me to sleep.

5. The next morning, our family awoke to a cold house and a silvery world outside. Ice coated everything. Cars left outside overnight lost all definition beneath the ice, their parts blended, forming one large ice sculpture. Hydro and telephone poles were wrapped in crystal armour, wires sagging between them like a knight's armour-clad arms. The scene reminded me of a lost world from a science-fiction story. I wanted to get out and touch the ice, slide my mittened hand over our railing and, of course, slide on the ice-covered snow.

6. Against my protests, my parents did not budge. My brother Ron and I remained inside while my parents called family to see how the storm had affected them. Only my grandparents had power, so it was decided that we would make our way there as soon as the streets were salted.

7. On our drive over later that morning, we travelled through an eerie ice-clad landscape. It was quiet and there were few people about. The occasional adventurer could be seen chopping and hacking away at the ice on their steps or their cars, but most people waited. At one point we came to a police blockade. They had closed some streets and we had to follow a detour. Our usual route had come alive with wires crisscrossing the road. Mom was quite

nervous and thought it might be better to go back home. Dad continued along and we finally got to Nanny's house. Two of my uncles had also returned because their homes were without electricity.

8. The rest of the day was spent hanging around, playing cards, eating, and listening to the radio. Reports told of major power outages in many areas of the province and of treacherous roads. The ice was 3 to 6 centimetres thick, and not only did it pull down hydro lines, it caused roofs to collapse. Throughout the afternoon, reports of damage grew. The TV was turned on briefly to catch some news but the reception was poor, so off it went. It felt like a great adventure. Everyone talked and laughed, and the children were occupied with card games, as the elements wreaked their havoc. I hoped it could continue for days and we'd be shut in like the pioneers.

9. Late that afternoon, when it was announced that all schools would be closed the next day, all of the children cheered. After supper, my mom called our neighbour who had decided to wait out the power failure and apparently it had just been restored. We waited about an hour; called back to make certain the electricity was still on; then went home.

10. Each February, I recall that ice storm and the togetherness and adventure that we shared when nature slowed us down and life became simple again.

Questions

1. Why do you think the author begins by discussing family get-togethers?

2. What ingenious method did Richard's father and uncles have for dealing with the freezing rain?

3. What different reactions did Richard and his parents have to the storm the next morning?

4. How did Richard probably feel on the ride to his grandparents' house? How did his mother feel?

5. Why does Richard describe the day as a "great adventure"?

6. What news did the children receive that made them very happy?

7. What special feeling did the ice storm evoke in Richard?

B   Find synonyms for the following words.

paragraph 1: got together

paragraph 6: electricity

paragraph 2: smells

paragraph 7: barrier

paragraph 3: attached

paragraph 4: calmed, quieted *lulled*

paragraph 8: busy

paragraph 9: evidently

paragraph 5: shape *definition*

paragraph 10: the weather

LANGUAGE AND CULTURE

Work in a group and discuss how these references are typical of the Canadian experience.

1.   the tango and the cha-cha

2.   a silvery world outside

3.   hydro and telephone poles wrapped in crystal armour

4.   salting the streets

5.   power outages

6.   the elements wreaked their havoc

7.   shut up like pioneers

WRITE ABOUT IT

One Fine Day...

Is the experience described in the story uniquely Canadian, or could it happen in other places?

Write about an experience you had that was related to the weather. It can be an experience from Canada or from another place you know.

WHAT IS CANADIAN CULTURE?

Discuss these questions in a group.

1. Many Canadians feel there are differences between being Canadian and being American. What do you think these differences are?

2. What similarities or differences would you notice between English speakers from the United States, Canada, Britain, or Australia?

3. Do you think people in Newfoundland have experiences and ideas that are similar to those of people in Saskatchewan, Quebec, or British Columbia?

4. How might music, art, or recreation differ across Canada, from east to west?

5. How much are people in Canada influenced by American culture such as music, movies, and magazines?

CANADIAN CAPSULES

In a recent poll, nearly three-quarters of Canadians said they believe Canadian culture is different from the culture of the United States. They said that Canadian history, geography, political systems, and treatment of minorities contribute to those differences.

CULTURAL ICONS

A Canada boasts many talented people who have created music, song, dance, art, and literature. Here is a list of some of these people and groups. With a partner, talk about the ones you know. Then answer the questions that follow.

Margaret Atwood	Robertson Davies
Leonard Cohen	Susan Aglukark
Sarah McLachlan	Michael J. Fox
Karen Kain	Mary Pickford
Alanis Morissette	William Shatner
Tragically Hip	Dan Aykroyd
Celine Dion	Alice Munro
Bruce Cockburn	Anne Murray
James Kudelka	Stephen Leacock
Melissa Etheridge	Margaret Laurence
Jackson Beardy	Irving Layton
Donald Sutherland	k.d. lang
Lynn Johnston	Oscar Peterson
Crash Test Dummies	Dennis Lee
Moist	Mordecai Richler
Linda Evangelista	Emily Carr
Alannah Myles	Michael Ondaatje

B   From the list in Exercise A, find the following:

1. a short male actor who has appeared in several popular American television series

2. a famous jazz musician

3. three rock groups

4. an actor in the popular series "Star Trek"

5. a songwriter and poet who is more famous in Europe than in North America

6. a movie actor who frequently plays humorous characters

7. a woman writer who has written many books of short stories and novels

8. a woman who blends country music with blues and pop, and frequently dresses like a man

9. a writer of best-selling novels who won an international literary prize for the novel *Alias Grace*

10. an award-winning poet best known for his children's verses

11. the world-famous author of humorous books who was a professor at McGill University

12. one of Canada's most successful and popular ballerinas

13. the winner of over 25 Juno awards and several Grammy Awards for songs such as "Snowbird"

14. a novelist who caused a stir when he wrote about his political views of Quebec

15. one of Canada's most famous artists, who painted nature and Aboriginal themes

16. a singer who used his music to draw attention to the plight of the Aboriginal peoples and the environment

17. a female cartoonist who represents family situations and is featured in dozens of newspapers worldwide

18. an actor who appeared in the movie version of "Mash"

19. a writer whose novel *The English Patient* was made into an academy-award-winning movie

20. a famous singer from Quebec who has won both Grammy and Juno awards

21. three female rock stars

22. an internationally famous fashion model from Canada

23. a writer as famous for his beard as for his literature

C   Check your answers at the end of the unit on page 22.

Present Perfect Continuous

There are two aspects to the present perfect: the perfective aspect and the continuous aspect. The perfective aspect suggests that two times (past and present) are involved. First you express the perfective aspect by using **have** + the past participle of **be** (**been**).

> She **has been...**

Then you express the continuous aspect by using the present participle of the main verb.

> She has been **studying** English since high school.

1. The present perfect continuous can be used to describe an action that began in the past, is progressive, and is still continuing.

> They **have been living** in the neighbourhood for years. (They still are.)

2. The present perfect continuous can also be used to show that an action that was going on has finished in the immediate past.

> They **have been painting** the living room. (It's a different colour and we can see the cans of paint and the ladders.)

 Rewrite these sentences using the present perfect continuous form of the verb.

1. John is managing an all-night gas station.

2. Suzanne is training for the Olympic Games.

3. Maria is teaching swimming at the YWCA.

4. Lili and Chen are renting an apartment downtown.

5. Max and Bob are building a boat in the basement.

6. The government is trying to discourage smoking.

7. Our school is offering scholarships to good students.

8. My grandmother is baking cookies for the bazaar on Saturday.

9. Julia is taking a French course this summer.

10. Marta is sewing a dress for her younger sister.

  B   Look at the pictures and answer the questions on page 20 with full sentences.

1. What have they been doing?	6. What has he been doing?
2. What have they been doing?	7. What has she been doing?
3. What has he been doing?	8. What have they been doing?
4. What have they been doing?	9. What has she been doing?
5. What has she been doing?	10. What have they been doing?

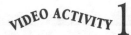

YAOHAN MARKET

VIDEO ACTIVITY 1

A   Watch the video. Summarize the information by answering the following questions:

1. What background information is given on the Yaohan market?

2. What are the main differences between old Chinatown in Vancouver and the new shopping centre?

3. What are some special products and departments in the Yaohan Market that we don't see in other Canadian supermarkets?

4. What changes would Ted Chao like to see in sources for his produce?

5. How did Laxman Naku adapt his farm to meet new market conditions?

6. How has immigration changed customs and habits in Vancouver?

B   Give your opinion of the issues raised in the video. Discuss these questions.

1. Have you ever lived in a community that has changed very quickly?

2. What do you think will happen if the Yaohan market opens other stores in Vancouver?

3. What are some of the big ethnic communities in other parts of Canada?

4. What impact do you think immigration from Hong Kong has had on the community in Vancouver?

CANADIAN CAPSULES

Many Canadians think of themselves as tolerant, peace-loving, and less violent than their American neighbours.

WRITE ABOUT IT

A Cultural Mosaic

Canada is a cultural mosaic with a harsh climate but a comfortable lifestyle. How do you feel about the country? Write about one of the following topics.

a) What Being Canadian Means to Me

   or

b) My Impressions of Canada

PERFECT YOUR ENGLISH

Land of Ice and Snow

Language reflects our culture, the things we find important and the things we do or don't discuss. In every language, there is a rich vocabulary to describe the things that are important to the people of that culture. For example, Arabic has several words to describe the horses or camels people once used for transportation. English has a variety of words to describe modes of transport: van, bus, streetcar, taxi, or jeep. Australian English has several words to describe sand.

The Inuit who live in Canada's Arctic have many words to describe snow and almost as many to describe ice. For the Inuit, knowing about snow and ice is important. For example, information about the quality and texture of the snow tells them about hunting and travelling conditions. As a result, the Inuit language has different words to describe not only snow on the ground, but also snow that is still falling or blowing with the wind. Here are a few of the many terms the Inuit use to describe snow:

- a snow flake: quannik
- melting snow: mannguqq
- the first snowfall of autumn: apinngaut
- soft snow on the ground: maujaq
- compressed and frozen snow: aniugaviniq
- blowing snow: piqtuluk
- falling wet snow: masak
- snow on the ground: aputi
- sparkling snow: pataqun

If something comes up from under the snow, the Inuit say: "Hatqummiqtuq!"

A   Work in a group. Make a list of several words to describe each of the following:

1.   a kind of entertainment (for example, movies)

2.   a weather condition (for example, rain)

3.   a type of food (for example, vegetables)

4.   a type of object commonly used (for example, a writing instrument)

5.   types of crimes (for example, white-collar crimes)

How many words can you think of in each case? How does this reflect our society's interest, or lack of interest, in this subject?

B   What is important in your language and culture? Can you think of any subject that has many words to describe it? List some of the words and describe the differences among them.

AT LAST

Now that you have finished the unit, go back to the activity "What's Your Take On This?" and discuss the questions again.

CULTURAL ICONS

Answers to Activity B (page 17)

1.   Michael J. Fox

2.   Oscar Peterson

3.   Tragically Hip, Crash Test Dummies, Moist

4.   William Shatner

5.   Leonard Cohen

6.   Dan Aykroyd

7.   Alice Munro

8.   k.d. lang

9.   Margaret Atwood

10.   Dennis Lee

11.   Stephen Leacock

12.   Karen Kain

13.   Anne Murray

14.   Mordecai Richler

15.   Emily Carr

16.   Bruce Cockburn

17.   Lynn Johnston

18.   Donald Sutherland

19.   Michael Ondaatje

20.   Celine Dion

21.   Alanis Morissette, Melissa Etheridge, Alannah Myles

22.   Linda Evangelista

23.   Robertson Davies

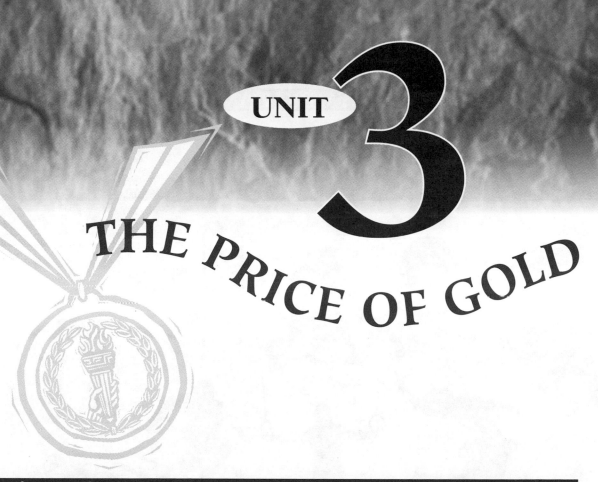

THE PRICE OF GOLD

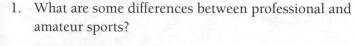

WHAT'S YOUR TAKE ON THIS?

Pain and Glory

Discuss these questions in a group.

1. What are some differences between professional and amateur sports?

2. What motivates top athletes to spend long hours in training for their sports?

3. Do you agree or disagree with the adage, "It's not important if you win or lose, but only how you play the game"?

4. How significant is the psychological element as opposed to the physical element in Olympic competition?

5. Why do we value "team players"?

6. If you were in pain but your participation was needed by your team, would you make an extra effort to continue?

7. At what point should a competitive athlete withdraw from competition because of pain or injury?

8. What do professional athletes do to continue playing when they are injured?

THE OLYMPIC GAMES

A In pairs, look at the silhouettes and identify the Olympic sports.

B Work in a group to discuss the list below. With which sports and countries do you associate these Olympic athletes?

Sylvie Frechette	Mark Spitz
Nancy Kerrigan	Donovan Bailey
Eleanor Holm	Elvis Stojko
Nadia Comaneci	Emil Zatopek
Johnny Weissmuller	Katarina Witt
Paavo Nurmi	Henry Hershkowitz
Kristin Otto	Dan Jensen
Ben Johnson	Alberto Juantorena
Yanmei Zhang	Greg Louganis

C Work in groups. Read the information and match each description to an athlete listed in Exercise B.

1. He disgraced his country when it was discovered he had used illegal drugs to boost his record-breaking performance in the 100 metres.

2. She was deprived of first place in her event when a judge made a scoring error, but was later awarded the gold medal in synchronized swimming.

3. She was the first gymnast to be awarded a perfect score of 10 for her performance in the Olympics.

4. He won gold in men's figure-skating for Canada.

5. In 1988, she became the first woman to win six gold medals in one Olympics.

6. She won the woman's figure-skating gold with a stunning and emotional performance of Carmen in Calgary.

7. This Israeli marksman survived the massacre of 11 team members at the Munich Olympics.

8. He won three gold medals in swimming, but later became more famous playing Tarzan in the movies.

9. He won a gold medal in Atlanta to redeem his country's reputation in the 100 metres.

10. This long-distance runner from Finland won nine gold medals.

11. This American swimmer set a world record by winning seven gold medals in a single Olympics.

12. He was the first runner to win the 400 metres and 800 metres in the same Olympics in Montreal.

13. This diver won gold in both the 3-metre springboard and 10-metre platform events in Seoul.

14. This speed-skater pursued the gold hours after hearing that his sister had died from leukemia.

15. A fellow figure-skater's plot to disable this skater had the world waiting for further developments.

16. In 1932, this glamorous swimmer won a gold medal and was then ordered off the team for drinking champagne.

17. This short-track speed-skater stormed off the victory podium in the middle of the award ceremony because she was infuriated by the rough tactics of the 500-metre winner from the United States.

18. In 1952, this Czechoslovakian runner won the 5000- and 10 000-metre races and the marathon.

When you have finished, check the answers at the end of the unit (page 37).

  D Answer these questions for yourself and then exchange information with your partners.

1. Can you name three Olympic medalists who come from your country?

2. Which sports did they play?

3. Which Olympic Games do you associate them with?

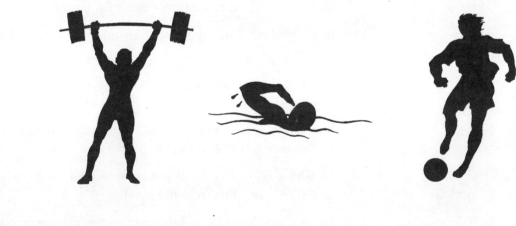

CANADIAN CAPSULES

In Canada and many other countries, athletes qualify for the Olympics by winning in competitions called "selection trials." Athletes are invited to participate in these trials based on their recent performance.

GOING FOR GOLD

A   This article contains a strong point of view. Skim the article and choose the best subtitle.

a)   Gymnast's health should have been priority

b)   Gymnast's courage deserves a nation's praise

Going For Gold

Bill Benner

1.   As Americans, should we be proud or ashamed, rejoice or be terribly, terribly sad? Tuesday night's conclusion to the women's gymnastics competition was either one of America's best Olympic moments or one of its worst. I'm probably in the minority, but I'm inclined to go with the latter.

2.   Today, little Kerri Strug is being praised as an American hero. Though it turned out not to be the case, it appeared the US gymnasts needed Strug's second and final vault to win the team Olympic gold medal—America's first in the event—Tuesday night in Atlanta's Georgia Dome. Vault, she did. Win, the Americans did.

3.   But at what cost? After her first vault, the girl was hurt. Badly. She landed badly, jamming her ankles and falling as she did. "I felt something snap," she would say afterwards. What snapped were two ligaments in her left ankle, X-rays later would reveal. The pain was obvious. It showed instantly on her contorted face and in her eyes.

4.   But when she looked to the sidelines for help and comfort, all she heard was encouragement. There was another vault left, another vault on which to get a higher score,

another vault to win that gold medal…or so it was believed. Talk about peer pressure. Strug was left with virtually no choice in her personal well-being. She had been programmed for this moment and she was to follow that time-honoured American tradition.

5.   Play with pain, just like the football players do. Remember though, some of those football players at least get the benefit of a syringe full of numbing Novocaine. So instead of some responsible adult grabbing this little girl, embracing her in a comforting hug, saying to her that her health isn't worth all the gold— let alone gold medals—in the world, she was urged to continue. No concern for her. Only concern for that medal.

6.   "Shake it off!" bellowed her coach, Bela Karolyi. "You can do it. You can do it. Go, go, go!" Coming from a man such as Karolyi, the most compelling figure in her life outside of her parents, this wasn't a plea. It was a command. We should not be surprised that Karolyi would be so inclined. In the name of gold medals, he has been exploiting—some would say abusing—young girls for a long time. He has, in fact, made a career of it. He is big Bela, and the little ones are putty in his hands. He moulds them. And

➡

if he breaks a few along the way, well, so be it. They'll heal…eventually…maybe.

7.   So Strug gamely limped to the end of the runway. She steeled herself, said a little prayer, ran and vaulted again. When she landed, all of America celebrated. The Georgia Dome crowd thundered its approval.

8.   They should have winced and gasped. It was a sickening sight watching her hop on one leg like a flamingo, then finally collapse in a heap. In the background, a judge covered her face with her hands. Strug was loaded on a stretcher, crying. NBC stuck a microphone in her face. "I had to do it," Strug said. Commentator John Tesh called her an inspiration. For whom? Every orthopedic surgeon in America?

9.   A short time later, Strug reappeared, carried in Bela's big arms. He offered her up like a sacrifice to the gods of Olympus. Karolyi said later that of all the gymnasts he thought capable of playing with pain, Strug would have been one of his last choices. She had surprised him. And now he carried her out and propped her up on the podium, like a prized piece of meat on a platter. She hadn't won for herself. She hadn't won for America. She had won for Bela.

10.   Someone hung a gold medal around Strug's neck. They played "The Star Spangled Banner." Strug's chest heaved. She cried not— I suspect—because of the significance of the occasion, but because her ankle was killing her. NBC played the Olympic theme, "The Power of the Dream," as it showed Strug grimacing in pain, crying. The power of this dream had been so strong it had lured a youngster into putting injury on top of injury.

11.   Yes, it was a dramatic moment. Yes, it made for terrific television—which is all that the IOC organizers want—even though this vault wasn't necessary for the US to win, as NBC led its audience to believe. Kerri Strug is a hero. An inspiration. A gold medalist. Even her father Burt, got caught up in the moment. "She showed what courage is all about," he said. "She put the team before herself."

12.   If that had been my daughter, I would have punched Bela Karolyi in his big fat face. I know, I know. How Mr. Strug raises his daughter is his business. I just think that you ought to be an adult—or a soldier—before you're encouraged to jump on the grenade. And one last question. They shoot horses, don't they?

    B   Work with a partner. Discuss the answers to these questions.

1.   What does the author mean when he says that Kerri Strug's win was either "one of America's best Olympic moments, or one of its worst"?

2.   What does the term "time-honoured American tradition" refer to?

3.   Compare Kerri's situation with that of a professional football player.

4.   Why did Kerri listen to Bela Karolyi?

5.   What reputation does Karolyi have?

6.   Why was Kerri called an inspiration?

7.   Why does the author think the crowd should have "winced and gasped"?

8.   Why does the author describe Kerri as being "carried and propped up on the podium liked a prized piece of meat on a platter"?

9.   What does the author mean when he says he would have punched Karolyi in the face?

10.   What do you think the author thinks Kerri's father should have done?

C Identify the following statements as **facts** or **opinions**.

1. Today little Kerri Strug is being praised as an American hero.

2. After the first vault, the girl was hurt.

3. It was a sickening sight watching her hop on one leg like a flamingo.

4. John Tesh called her an inspiration.

5. I just think that you ought to be an adult before you're encouraged to jump on the grenade.

6. Her health isn't worth all the gold—or gold medals—in the world.

7. We should not be surprised that Karolyi would encourage her to jump.

8. The power of this dream had been so strong it had lured a youngster into putting injury on top of injury.

9. This vault wasn't necessary for the US to win.

10. NBC played "The Power of the Dream" as it showed Strug grimacing in pain, crying.

D Identify the following words with either the **public's** interpretation of the event or the **author's** interpretation. Write **P** or **A** for each word.

1. praise
2. exploiting
3. abusing
4. approval
5. inspiration
6. sacrifice
7. lured
8. sickening
9. courage
10. celebrated
11. hero
12. grimacing
13. proud
14. ashamed
15. rejoice

CANADIAN CAPSULES

Political conflicts have led to boycotts of the Olympic Games on several occasions. About 30 nations withdrew their teams from the 1976 Games in Montreal because of political disputes.

LANGUAGE AND CULTURE

Work in a group and discuss the meaning of these expressions.

1. the Georgia Dome

2. peer pressure

3. a syringe full of numbing Novocaine

4. Shake it off.

5. The little ones are putty in his hands.

6. She steeled herself.

7. He propped her up on the podium.

8. "The Star Spangled Banner"

9. to jump on the grenade

10. They shoot horses, don't they?

WRITE ABOUT IT

How Far Would You Go?

Do you agree or disagree with the author's point of view in the article on Kerri Strug? Choose one of the titles below and write about your point of view.

a) Gymnast's health should have been the priority.

or

b) Gymnast's courage deserves a nation's praise.

 **Past Perfect**

The past perfect relates two times in the past to describe two actions in the past when one occurred before the other.

Use the auxiliary verb **had** + the past participle of the main verb. Use the simple past for the action in the more recent past and the past perfect for the action earlier in the past. **Already** is often used with the past perfect.

> The team **had already won** the competition when Kerri **made** her last vault.

A Choose the correct verb and put it in the past perfect with **already**.

**have be married win eat go turn down be leave
play stop**

1. Jack _____ many competitions when they selected him for the team.

2. When we phoned to complain about the noise, they _____ the music.

3. Most of the other players _____ home when we got to the practice.

4. We _____ dinner when the girls came home from the pool.

5. When we got to the tennis court, the contestants _____ the first match.

6. When the alarm clock rang, Joseph _____ awake for nearly an hour.

7. The customer _____ the store when the clerk noticed a mistake in the bill.

8. The doctor _____ the bleeding when the ambulance arrived.

9. My grandparents _____ three children when my mother was born.

10. Susan and Mike _____ for five or six years when we first met them.

Past Perfect + "By the Time"

By the time means at the moment a past action took place or before that point in time. Use **by the time** in the clause with the simple past tense. Use the past perfect with the main clause.

A Combine the following pairs of sentences using **by the time**.

> We got to the stadium. The game had started.
>
> **By the time we got to the stadium, the game had started.**

1. She waited in the rain for 15 minutes. The bus finally arrived.

2. They had played 18 holes of golf. It started to rain.

3. The paramedics had finished their work. The ambulance arrived.

4. He had lived in several different countries. He decided to settle in Canada.

5. She lost her title. She had been national champion for six years.

6.   We had finished our warm-up exercises. The coach came out of the dressing room.

7.   My appetizer came to the table. Everyone else had finished theirs.

8.   He earned his black belt. He had studied karate for five years.

9.   She learned to speak Japanese. She had been in Japan for a year.

10. My friends had all gone home. I finally left the library.

SILKEN LAUMANN'S GOLD MEDAL

LISTENING ACTIVITY 2

A Read these paragraphs for background information.

Silken Laumann was a member of Canada's Olympic rowing team. Three months before the Olympic Games in Barcelona, the young woman from Victoria, BC, was involved in a training accident where she suffered a serious injury to her leg. Because of her remarkable physical condition and determination, Laumann was able to defy the odds and participate in the Olympics. Despite her injury, she won a bronze medal in the Barcelona Olympic Games.

Determined to go for gold, the young rower continued to train and participate in international competitions. Laumann's hard work and determination finally paid off when she and her team mates won gold medals during the Pan American Games in Mar del Plata, Argentina. But it seemed that gold was not only hard to get but hard to keep! Through a strange quirk of fate, it looked as if Silken Laumann's gold medal would be lost.

B Listen to the tape. Summarize the information by answering these questions in a group.

1. What were the circumstances that led to Silken Laumann's troubles with Pan American Games rules?

2. Why did Caroline Lethran offer her unqualified support to Silken?

3. What was the official position of the Canadian Olympic Committee?

4. What arguments did the people at the Toronto sports club and Laumann's colleague in Victoria give to counteract the idea she had deliberately taken a banned substance?

5. What was the final outcome of the case?

  C Give your opinion of the issues raised on the tape. Discuss these questions in a group.

1. How do you think Silken Laumann felt?

2. If you were her team-mate and were stripped of a gold medal, how would you feel?

3. Do you think the decision was fair given the circumstances?

4. Why do you think the Pan American Games Committee made the decision it did?

5. Do you think the decision would have encouraged Laumann to give up competitive sports? Why or why not?

PERFECT YOUR ENGLISH

Sports and Business

The following idiomatic expressions come from the world of sports, especially baseball and football. Since business—like sports—was, for a long time, the domain of men, these expressions have found their way from the locker room to the boardroom.

  A Read the expressions. Which sport do you associate with each?

1. to get to first base
2. a ballpark figure
3. to go the distance
4. to play ball
5. to tackle a problem
6. to be way out in left field
7. a heavyweight
8. to be out of bounds
9. a whole new ball game

10. to go to bat for someone
11. to throw in the towel
12. to be a team player
13. to take the ball and run with it
14. to strike out
15. to pinch-hit for someone
16. to beat someone to the punch
17. to score points with someone
18. to touch base with someone

B   What do the idioms mean on Bay Street? Match the meanings below to the expressions on page 35.

a) to act improperly or illegally

b) to stand up for someone else

c) to impress someone favourably

d) to accomplish the first step towards a goal

e) to miss the point completely

f) a rough estimate

g) to check in with a colleague

h) to take on a difficult problem

i) to give up on negotiations suddenly

j) to substitute for someone else

k) to persevere until you succeed

l) to act before someone else has time to

m) to agree to participate

n) to work well with others

o) someone with a lot of power

p) to fail in your objective

q) to take over a project and move it ahead rapidly

r) a completely new set of circumstances

AT LAST

Now that you have finished the unit, go back to the activity "What's Your Take On This?" and discuss the questions again.

CANADIAN CAPSULES

The illegal use of drugs was a serious problem in the 1988 Summer Olympics, when ten athletes were disqualified because they used banned substances to enhance their performances. Canadian sprinter Ben Johnson lost his gold medal when routine tests revealed a banned substance in his system.

THE OLYMPIC GAMES

Answers to Activity C (page 27)

1. Ben Johnson
2. Sylvie Frechette
3. Nadia Comaneci
4. Elvis Stojko
5. Kristin Otto
6. Katarina Witt
7. Henry Hershkowitz
8. Johnny Weissmuller
9. Donovan Bailey
10. Paavo Nurmi
11. Mark Spitz
12. Alberto Juantorena
13. Greg Louganis
14. Dan Jensen
15. Nancy Kerrigan
16. Eleanor Holm
17. Yanmei Zhang
18. Emil Zatopek

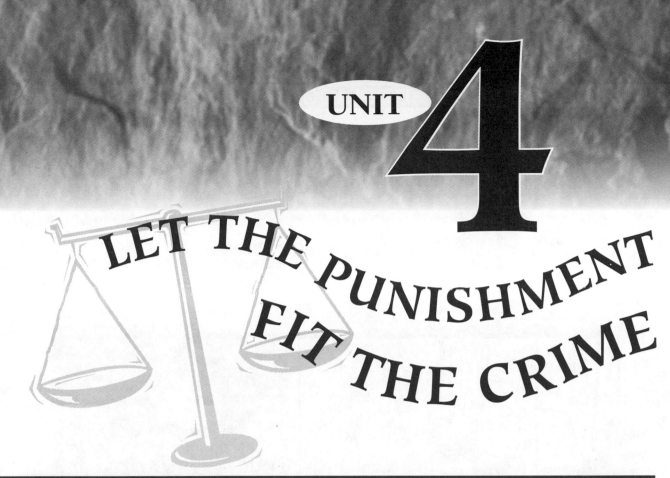

LET THE PUNISHMENT FIT THE CRIME

WHAT'S YOUR TAKE ON THIS?

Is Crime Out of Control?

Work in groups to discuss these questions.

1. Do you think crime is increasing in our society?

2. What is the purpose of the sentences handed out in courts of law?

3. Would stricter punishments by the courts deter criminals?

4. Do you believe in capital punishment for certain kinds of crime?

5. If so many criminals come out of jail and return to criminal activities, what is wrong with our prison system?

6. Do you think that all offenders should be treated the same way by the courts?

YOU BE THE JUDGE

A   Work in a group. Put these crimes in order from most to least serious.

robbery   fraud

assault   drug dealing

vandalism   drunk driving

car theft   burglary

manslaughter   kidnapping

attempted murder   forgery

B   What sentences would you impose for each of the crimes above? Specify years of imprisonment, amount of fines, method of capital punishment, or other punishments.

DOES THE PUNISHMENT FIT THE CRIME?

Which of the statements below do you associate with each of the stories that follow? Statements can match more than one story.

1. Capital punishment is an uncertain deterrent.

2. Prison terms don't seem to be working.

3. Society has a right to be warned about known criminals.

4. Australia's original settlers were considered criminals.

5. Jail isn't the only way to deal with criminals.

6. The justice system isn't effective in dealing with criminals.

7. Criminals need to understand the effects of their crimes.

8. Sending criminals away is one way of protecting society.

9. Criminals should be ashamed of what they have done.

A The Pickpocket Story

Some people have argued that severe punishments deter crime. In seventeenth-century England, it was customary to hang pickpockets. A hanging was a major public event where people gathered around the scaffold to watch the execution. While the crowd looked up at the scaffold, pickpockets would work through the gathering, stealing people's valuables while they were distracted.

B The Shaming Judge

With a crime wave sweeping Florida and criminals leaving and returning to prison as though caught in a revolving door, one judge has had an idea. Rather than systematically sending criminals to jail, he has begun imposing "shaming" sentences as deterrents. A vandal, for example, had to place a signed ad in the newspaper apologizing for the damage he had caused to public property. A child molester had to post a sign on his house warning children to stay away. The judge hopes this type of sentence will deter criminals from committing new crimes.

C   Transportation

When people left the countryside and moved to cities in large numbers in eighteenth-century England, one result was a large number of unemployed and hungry people. A crime wave followed. How did the courts react? They began to sentence people to "transportation." Judges sent many people—even children—off in ships to a penal colony across the world. Even people who committed minor crimes, such as stealing a loaf of bread, could be sent to the British penal colony in Australia.

JUSTICE WITHOUT COURTROOMS

A   Discuss these questions.

1. Have you ever been victim of a crime?

2. How did you feel about the person who committed the crime?

3. Would you want to meet a person who had committed an offence against you, face to face?

4. Do you think victims should have a role in sentencing offenders?

5. Do you think prison is an effective punishment for criminals?

B   Scan the article for the answers to these questions.

1. What was the crime in this story?

2. Who were the victims?

3. Who were the offenders?

4. What was the outcome?

People in Canada have different ideas about how to deal with crime. Some people believe criminals should be rehabilitated, while others believe that punishment should be used as a deterrent.

Justice Without Courtrooms

Debbie Parkes

1. Isabelle Gosselin still gets emotional about the break-in at her family's home. It was in the month of October. The family had moved in only 12 days earlier. Gosselin and her husband stood staring at a disaster zone: orange juice and ketchup splattered on the fresh white walls, plants overturned, toys thrown about and broken, the television and stereo missing. "How could anyone be so mean?" their daughter Josianne, 7 at the time, tearfully asked.

2. The next day was spent with police, an insurance adjuster, alarm-installers, a cleaning company. For months after, Josianne would wake up with nightmares. "I felt pretty discouraged," recalled Gosselin. There were times, she said, when she would just sit down and cry.

3. About a year went by and Gosselin and her husband heard nothing from police. Then suddenly an organization that works with young offenders in their region called Gosselin's home. Two teenagers had been charged with a series of local break-ins, including the one at Gosselin's home. The trial of one youth was still pending but the other youth—aged 15 at the time of the break-in—had been found guilty, the worker added.

4. The youth worker on the phone explained that his organization's mandate is to oversee the carrying out of alternative sentences for youths. Probably the best-known alternative sentence is the requirement to do community work. But in the case of the youth who broke into the Gosselin's home, the youth worker writing up the pre-sentence report wanted to recommend something less well-known: victim-offender mediation, where the two parties meet to talk about how the incident affected them and try to work out a settlement acceptable to both sides. Mediation is an option only if both sides agree.

5. It was the first time Gosselin had heard of victim-offender mediation. But she sensed it would be a good experience for her. For one thing, she could tell the young offender face to face just how much he had hurt her family. For another, she could get answers to some of the questions that had been bothering her for months: What would the offender have done if the family had been home? Had he been armed?

6. For more than a decade, victim-offender mediation has been promoted as a fairer and more meaningful form of justice for both offender and victim. "We're looking for something that resembles an Aboriginal form of justice where people sit down together to resolve their conflicts," says the criminologist who co-ordinates the group. Only one or two victims in 100 refuse mediation when the process is properly explained to them, he said. "However, it is important that mediation not be presented as therapy for the youth; there must be equal concern for the victim. Victims are doubly victimized if they are used for therapeutic reasons."

➡

7.   The few studies that have been done on the effect of mediation indicate that it helps reduce the rate of recidivism. The goal of mediation shouldn't be to reduce recidivism in order to save taxpayers money, but to provide a fairer, more humane form of justice—one that looks at how to make the situation right for both parties, experts say.

8.   "For the young person, it's something that makes a lot of sense," explains one youth worker. "It's one of the best ways to make him understand the harm he has done." Offenders depersonalize their victims, which prevents the offender from feeling empathy, criminologists and psychologists note. Another benefit of mediation is that the young offender gets to feel part of the justice process. Too often, offenders feel like victims of the court system and emerge from the system angrier than when they went in, compelling them to commit other crimes.

9.   In addition, the crime victims often feel as victimized by the judicial process as they were by the original offence. They are frustrated by rules of evidence that seen to protect the offender more than the victim, by prison terms that do nothing to repair the damage caused by the offence. "Most of the time, the victims find out that the crime wasn't premeditated. That's reassuring for the victim. They think, 'OK, the offender had nothing against me personally,'" remarks one youth worker. In Gosselin's case, she found out her house was chosen at random, the youths weren't armed, and had someone been home they would have pretended they were calling on a friend but had got the wrong house.

10.   The first step after the victim and the offender have been contacted by phone is for mediators to meet with them individually to explain how the process works. A few days later, the victim and the offender are brought in for a joint meeting. They are accompanied by two mediators—a centre employee and a volunteer who is there as a symbol of the community's involvement. The victim and the offender sit across from each other at a table, with the mediators at the other ends.

11.   The young person gives his version of what happened and answers any questions the victim might have. The victim describes the impact of the crime on his or her family. Then the victim and offender decide on an acceptable form of compensation. There are no rules on what this can be. Settlements have included everything from replacing the stolen item to painting a victim's fence. It's striking how often victims start off the process insisting they want to be fully compensated financially but end up satisfied with a simple apology.

12.   In Gosselin's case, her home-insurance policy had covered most of the damage. But one of her main concerns was to restore a sense of security for Josianne. Before heading for the mediation meeting, she told Josianne that the youth who had broken into their house must be a very unhappy person. Josianne said he was probably like Barracuda from a television program. Barracuda is a troubled kid who constantly gets into trouble but is a good person deep down.

13.   At the meeting, Gosselin told the youth how his and his friend's actions had affected the family in a way he could never imagine. But of everyone in the family Josianne had been affected the most. The youth had broken the girl's favourite piggy bank—Gosselin had made it for her daughter in a pottery class. And that Carmen Campagne CD he and his friend had trashed? Josianne had received it only two weeks earlier for her birthday.

14.   "I think it touched him a lot to realize that children were involved," Gosselin said. "He told me he wanted to have children himself one day and that he'd never meant to hurt a child." Then Gosselin said, she told the youth about Josianne's Barracuda comparison and that surely he had a streak of good in him. Gosselin suggested as a settlement, the youth buy Josianne Carmen Campagne's latest CD release. He agreed and a few days later he dropped the CD off. It came carefully wrapped. With it was a card that read: "Josianne, I'm very sorry for what I did and I hope you're not too angry with me." The youth had signed it "Barracuda."

C   Read the story and answer the questions.

1. What upset the child most about the break-in?

2. What did the Gosselins learn one year after the break-in?

3. What did the youth worker who spoke to Gosselin propose?

4. Why did Gosselin sense victim-offender mediation would be a good experience?

5. What is victim-offender mediation compared with?

6. Why is it important that the mediation not focus on rehabilitating the offender?

7. Explain why the justice system usually isn't effective for the offender or the victim.

8. What was Gosselin reassured to learn during mediation?

9. What are the steps in the mediation process?

10. What part of Gosselin's presentation touched the offender?

11. What compensation was offered in Gosselin's case?

12. Explain why the offender signed his name "Barracuda."

D   Use the words from the text to complete the puzzle.

Across

1. compensation (paragraph 14)

4. upset (paragraph 1)

7. criminals (paragraph 3)

8. felt (paragraph 5)

11. planned in advance (paragraph 9)

14. forcing (paragraph 8)

15. aim (paragraph 7)

Down

2. destroyed (paragraph 13)

3. bad dreams (paragraph 2)

5. Native (paragraph 6)

6. repeating crimes (paragraph 7)

9. choice (paragraph 4)

10. effect (paragraph 11)

12. disturbed (paragraph 12)

13. young person (paragraph 3)

GRAMMAR FOCUS — Gerunds vs. Infinitives

When one verb follows another in a sentence, the second verb has either a gerund or an infinitive form. Some verbs are followed by gerunds, some verbs are followed by infinitives, and some verbs can be followed by either a gerund or an infinitive.

> Gerund: He regretted **breaking** the child's toys.
>
> Infinitive: He agreed **to pay** compensation.
>
> Gerund or Infinitive: He proposed **paying** her back.
>
> He proposed **to pay** her back.

Some Verbs Used With Gerunds

admit	finish
avoid	keep
consider	regret
deny	stop
discuss	suggest
enjoy	understand

Some Verbs Used With Infinitives

agree	need
appear	prepare
ask	plan
choose	promise
decide	refuse
expect	seem
forget	threaten
happen	want
hope	wish

Some Verbs Used With Either

begin	prefer
continue	remember
hate	start
like	try
love	

A Choose the correct form of the verb in each sentence. Write **B** for sentences in which both forms are correct.

1. The judge refused (making/to make) an exception in the case.

2. The victim demanded (to get/getting) compensation from the robber.

3. The criminal tried (escaping/to escape) from the cell in the police station.

4. Someone in the family forgot (locking/to lock) the door before he or she left.

5. The man they arrested denied (being/to be) responsible for the crime.

6. One man admitted (entering/to enter) the house through the basement.

7. He chose (hiring/to hire) a well-known criminal lawyer to defend him.

8. Nobody enjoys (coming/to come) home and discovering a break-in.

9. The police finished (taking/to take) notes at the scene of the crime.

10. The teenage criminal started (crying/to cry) in front of the judge.

B Complete the following sentences with gerunds or infinitives.

1. The witness promised _____ (tell) the truth at the trial.

2. The suspect just happened _____ (be) at the scene.

3. No one enjoys _____ (appear) in a court of law.

4. Criminals usually avoid _____ (leave) fingerprints.

5. The police refused _____ (say) why they had arrived late.

6. The judge threatened _____ (force) the man to testify.

7. We hoped _____ (see) justice being done in court.

8. The lawyers discussed _____ (apply) for a new trial.

9. The prisoner seemed _____ (regret) what he had done.

10. No one expected _____ (hear) such a harsh sentence.

CANADIAN CAPSULES   The Fraser Region Community Justice Initiatives Association in Langley, BC, offers mediation between inmates and victims or their relatives for some major offences such as assault, rape, and murder.

ALTERNATIVE PUNISHMENT

 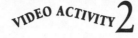

A Watch the video. Summarize the information by answering the questions below.

1. Kevin Hollinsky got into trouble. Why is his particular crime of such interest to the community?

2. What motivated Joey's and Andrew's parents to adopt the position they took when Kevin went to court?

3. What particularly influenced the judge in deciding on an alternative sentence?

4. What role did Joey's and Andrew's parents play when Kevin visited the schools?

5. What was the prosecutor's reason for wanting a jail sentence for Kevin?

6. What made the police officer change his mind about the sentence?

B Give your opinion of the issues raised in the video. Discuss these questions.

1. Do you think that Kevin's appearances at the schools were effective in deterring drinking and driving among the students?

2. After Kevin had talked to 8300 high school students, a psychologist recommended that he quit giving presentations because it was too hard on him. Do you think the punishment the judge imposed on Kevin was reasonable or unreasonable?

3. Do you think that Kevin will be able to live a useful, productive life in the future?

4. Do you think bars that serve alcohol to under-age people should be held responsible under the law?

5. Why do you think that drunk driving among teens is a problem of particular concern?

WRITE ABOUT IT

A Hard Choice

Write about one of these topics:

a) Kevin Hollinsky's case was not an easy one for the judge who had to sentence him. Why was the judge's decision so difficult?

or

b) What do you think should be done to reduce the amount of crime in today's society?

PERFECT YOUR ENGLISH

Spellbound

People say that it is difficult to master English spelling because there are so many exceptions to the rules. The writer George Bernard Shaw is one of many people who have proposed a simpler system of spelling. Shaw argued against continuing to use a system in which the word "fish" could equally well be spelled "ghoti." Think about it. The sound made by the letter "f" is often written "gh," as in the word "cough." The letter "o" can be pronounced as if it were an "i," as in the word "women." The letters "ti" could be pronounced "sh," as they are in the word "nation."

Shaw's comment is witty, but in reality there is a logical system of spelling in English—or in most of the English language, anyway. Eighty percent of words are straightforward. More than ten percent stick fairly closely to the rules. Unfortunately, the remaining words—the illogical ones—include many of the commonest or everyday words such as "done," "gone," and "of."

  A Work with a partner to practise pronouncing the following "problem" words.

1.	tough	11.	caught
2.	knight	12.	wind
3.	though	13.	houses
4.	thought	14.	ancient
5.	knit	15.	health
6.	lead	16.	clause
7.	answer	17.	close
8.	bough	18.	thorough
9.	listen	19.	rough
10.	earning	20.	major

B Pronounce this set of words. Write the words and circle the vowels. What do you notice?

bird   heard

word   herd

curd

C   Pronounce these homographs.

1. a) the wind
    b) to wind

2. a) a minute
    b) a minute quantity

3. a) read (present)
    b) read (past)

4. a) to live
    b) a live performance

5. a) to desert
    b) the desert

6. a) a present
    b) to present

7. a) an address
    b) to address

8. a) a record
    b) to record

AT LAST

 Now that you have finished the unit, go back to the activity "What's Your Take On This?" and discuss the questions again.

SMOKE SCREEN

WHAT'S YOUR TAKE ON THIS?

The Power of Persuasion

To begin the unit, work in a group to discuss these questions.

1. What types of messages appear on cigarette packages and cigarette advertisements?

2. Do you believe a person's opinion of smoking could be manipulated by advertising?

3. At which specific audiences do tobacco companies aim their ads?

4. What are some reasons why people choose to smoke cigarettes?

5. At what age do you think people generally start smoking?

6. Name some places where it is common to see cigarette advertising.

7. Why do you think governments are concerned about smoking?

LANGUAGE AND CULTURE

A   Look at the words in the box. Discuss what they mean.

lobbyist

misleading   propaganda

cover-up

advertising   alternative

disinformation   manipulation

B   Work with a partner to answer these questions.

1.   What is the difference between advertising and propaganda?

2.   What does a lobbyist do?

3.   Give an example of a "cover-up."

4.   What strategies do advertisers use to manipulate consumers?

5.   Which word in the box above matches this definition: "making someone believe something that is not true"?

6.   Which of the words in the box might describe a government ad promoting the Canada Food Guide?

7.   Which word in the box matches this definition: "false or misleading information issued in order to discredit someone or something"?

C   Match the product or kind of ad below with an image or slogan on page 55.

1.   Participaction

2.   beer

3.   eggs

4.   detergent

5.   Virginia Slims

6.   airlines

7.   cigarettes

8.   public service ads

9.   milk

a) a family practising some sport together

b) a group of men in a fishing cabin

c) "You've come a long way baby!"

d) a laid-back cowboy in the wide open spaces

e) little boys playing football in the mud

f) famous people wearing white mustaches

g) "Let's get crackin'"

h) tropical beaches

i) Notice: Adjust your clock to daylight savings time.

TO SMOKE OR NOT TO SMOKE?

Many airlines no longer allow smoking, some restaurants have "no smoking" policies, and cigarette packages carry dire warnings of the consequences to your health; yet smokers continue to smoke.

 Read these statements, which give people's reasons for smoking. Then work in pairs to answer the questions that follow.

a) They want to have a sophisticated image.

b) Friends smoke and they feel peer pressure.

c) It helps them relax and escape stress.

d) They don't want to gain weight.

e) It is easier to fit in at parties.

f) Advertising for cigarettes is very persuasive.

g) They have become addicted to nicotine.

h) They identify with sports events sponsored by tobacco companies.

1. Which of these statements apply to teenagers? Which apply to adults?

2. Which statements apply to people when they start smoking?

3. Which statements reflect reasons people give as excuses not to quit smoking?

4. How many of these reasons have you heard given as an excuse, and who has given them?

5. If you smoke or smoked in the past, have you used any of these reasons as an excuse yourself? If not, what reasons have you given?

DO TOBACCO ADS WORK ON TEENS?

A   Skim the article to find the following information.

1. Gilles Villeneuve's sponsor

2. the tobacco industry's "greatest salesman"

3. the age at which more than half of smokers start

4. why smoking is regarded as a pediatric disease

5. the two contradictory impulses of adolescents

6. the image that is most appealing to teenagers

7. the percentage of teens who have seen tobacco-sponsored ads

8. the brands smoked by 90 percent of young smokers

9. the cartoon character recognized by 91 percent of 6-year olds

10. the kind of influence more powerful than family or friends

11. what happened to Australian chidren who approved of cigarette ads

12. the reason smoking jumped among under-18-year-old girls

13. what influences an adult's choice of cigarette brands

Do Tobacco Ads Work On Teens?

Sarah Scott

1. Race-car driver Gilles Villeneuve has everything a teenage boy could hope for: a fast car, a high-speed risky life, and glittering international success. The girls adore him. Images of his childlike face were plastered all over the city during the Grand Prix car race last summer. You could hardly miss the name of his team's sponsor—Rothmans, the cigarette company.

2. Those images, anti-tobacco activists say, tell the story: Tobacco companies are aiming to snare teenagers in their nicotine trap. If teens want to be like Villeneuve, maybe they'll smoke the brand of cigarettes advertised on his helmet, anti-tobacco activists say. "He's the modern Marlboro Man," said an anti-smoking spokesperson. He was quoting a senior marketing executive at Philip Morris, the maker of Marlboro,

who said the allure of auto racing fits the rugged, individualistic, heroic image of the Marlboro Man, the tobacco industry's greatest-ever salesman.

3. Now the Canadian government wants to stop the tobacco companies from using teen idols like Villeneuve to sell their deadly products. Under legislation being studied by the Canadian Senate, tobacco companies won't be able to put up signs displaying their brand names for sponsored events—unless the signs are at the event site, in bars, or in newspapers read primarily by adults.

4. Canada, like the United States, is cracking down on teen smoking because almost all smokers take up the habit when they are teens, and half start before age 16. Smoking is regarded as a pediatric disease because hardly any adults

older than 20 become addicted to
cigarettes. Teen users are crucial to

...youthful smokers smoked either Du
...r... or Player's.

9. In the US, where there's no ban, 91 percent
of 6-year-olds and 3... percent of 3-year olds
recognized the Camel, the cartoon star of one
tobacco ad campaign. Among young children,
the Camel is as recognizable as Mickey Mouse.

10. Tobacco ads **might encourage some
kids to smoke.** A California study concluded
that adolescents who were "receptive" to
tobacco advertising were more likely to consider
... and offered one than
those who were not receptive to tobacco
advertising. The author... of the study said that
receptivity to ads was a more powerful influence
than friends and family.

11. An Australian study reported that
children aged 10 to 12 who approved of cigarette
ads were twice as likely to start smoking in the
next year than children who didn't approve of
the ads.

12. Smoking campaigns have had an
impact on kids in the past. Smoking among
... abruptly around 1967,
... American ... launched its "You've
come a long way, baby" campaign.

13. The US health department found
tobacco ads have a more profound effect on
brand choices by young people (86 percent of
young people smoke the most advertised
brands) than on adults, whose choice is more
often based on price.

B   Find words in the text that mean the same as the following.

1. posted (paragraph 1)	10. equilibrium (paragraph 6)
2. attraction (paragraph 2)	11. aiming at (paragraph 7)
3. tough (paragraph 2)	12. prepare (paragraph 7)
4. heroes (paragraph 3)	13. poll (paragraph 8)
5. mainly (paragraph 3)	14. prohibition (paragraph 9)
6. childhood (paragraph 4)	15. probable (paragraph 11)
7. addicted (paragraph 4)	16. began (paragraph 12)
8. urges (paragraph 5)	17. trademark (paragraph 13)
9. suggestions (paragraph 6)	

 **C**   Work in a group to discuss questions about the text on teen smoking.

1. Why do cigarette companies especially want to hook teenage smokers?

2. What image is projected by the brands that are most successful with teenagers?

3. How did so many children in the US become familiar with Joe Camel?

4. What do you think are the implications of the California study for the debate on tobacco advertising?

5. What caused a sharp increase in smoking by teenage girls around 1967?

6. Contrast the factors that affect brand choice among teens with those that affect adults.

GRAMMAR FOCUS   Conditional Sentences

A conditional sentence shows an **if/then** relationship between two actions. In conditional sentences, the tense of the **if** clause tells whether the condition expressed is probably going to happen, is very unlikely to happen, or did not happen.

Conditional I

Use Conditional I for real future possibility. Use the present tense in the **if** clause and the future tense in the main clause. The future tense in the main clause can be affirmative or negative.

A   Choose the correct clause to complete these sentences logically.

1. If you aren't careful,
   a) you won't get addicted.
   b) you'll get addicted.

2. If he smokes cigarettes in the restaurant,
   a) he'll bother the other customers.
   b) he won't bother the other customers.

3. If they don't hurry up,
   a) they won't be on time.
   b) they'll be on time.

4. If the smoking ads aren't regulated,
   a) health costs will increase.
   b) health costs won't increase.

5. If no one speaks up about tobacco ads,
   a) more teens will be hooked.
   b) more teens won't be hooked.

6. If you arrive at the office late,
   a) you'll find a parking spot easily.
   b) you won't find a parking spot easily.

7. If they don't hurry up,
   a) they won't be on time.
   b) they'll be on time.

8. If everyone drives carefully,
   a) there won't be an accident.
   b) there will be an accident.

9. If he doesn't stop smoking,
   a) it will affect his health.
   b) it won't affect his health.

10. If I don't know the answer,
    a) I'll put up my hand.
    b) I won't put up my hand.

Conditional II

Use Conditional II for hypothetical situations. Use the past tense in the **if** clause. The use of **would** with the main verb suggests that the situation is unreal (imaginary).

> If he continued to smoke, he would risk getting lung cancer.

A   Complete the sentences with the correct form of the verb in brackets.

1.   If I _____ (stop) smoking, I would gain a lot of weight.

2.   We would understand better, if you _____ (speak) more slowly.

3.   If the results of the study were clear, they _____ (pass) the bill.

4.   If I _____ (know) him better, I would introduce you.

5.   He _____ (win) more competitions if he practised harder.

6.   If she _____ (take) better care of herself, she would have fewer health problems.

7.   She would be a better friend if she _____ (not/break) her promises.

8.   Elena would probably feel better if she _____ (give up) cigarettes.

9.   If he saw the job advertised, he _____ (apply) for it.

10. They would buy a car if they _____ (have) enough money in the bank.

Conditional III

Use Conditional III (past unreal) for hypothetical or imaginary situations in the past. Use the past perfect form in the **if** clause. Use **would have** before the main verb.

If she **had known** cigarettes were addictive, she **would have avoided** them.

past condition that didn't occur   hypothetical situation that didn't occur

A   Match the short statements with the Conditional III sentences on page 61.

1.   I didn't know about his condition.

2.   He didn't know the way.

3.   She doesn't have good study habits.

4.   They did not provide good service.

5.   She was only there for three days.

6.   I didn't know about your plans.

7.   They were poor administrators.

8.   He tried to get into a well-known institution

9.   They couldn't afford food and accommodation any longer.

10. The cost of telephone calls was high.

a)   If I had known you were coming too, I would have waited.

b)   If he had applied to a less famous university, he would have been accepted.

c)   They wouldn't have gone bankrupt if they had managed the company better.

d)   If she had spent more time in Turkey, she would have looked you up.

e)   I would have been more gentle if I had known he was injured.

f)   If the hotel hadn't been so expensive, they would have stayed longer.

g)   He wouldn't have been late for the practice if he hadn't got lost.

h)   If she had had better study habits, she would have had higher marks.

i)   We would have called more often if the long distance rates had been lower.

j)   We wouldn't have lost our tempers if the clerk hadn't been so arrogant.

 B   Read the **if** clauses in the sentences above aloud with a partner. In what tense are the verb phrases in the **if** clauses?

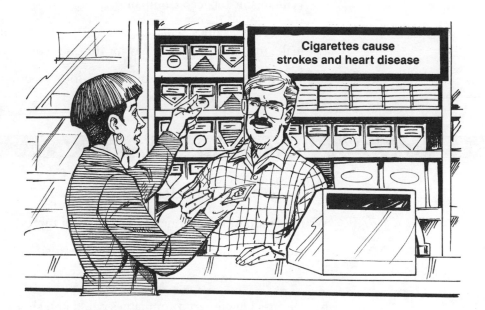

CANADIAN CAPSULES   Surveys indicate that, after declining steadily and then levelling off in the late '80s, teen smoking in Canada has gone up the '90s.

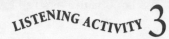

TOBACCO COMPANIES UNDER ATTACK

   LISTENING ACTIVITY 3

  A Discuss these questions in a group.

1. Why might tobacco companies be under attack?

2. Who might attack them and why?

3. How could tobacco companies defend themselves in the face of evidence that cigarettes cause serious health problems?

4. Who pays for the health problems that result from cigarette smoking?

 B Listen to the tape and answer the questions.

1. What charge is the head of the Food and Drug Agency making against cigarette companies?

2. How does the tobacco company executive respond to the accusation?

3. What is the reaction of the US Justice Department?

4. What charge does Dr. David Kessler make about the Brown and Williamson Tobacco Company?

5. What reasons does Senator Lautenburg give for introducing a bill to make tobacco companies pay for illnesses connected with smoking?

6. What is the ultimate goal of the anti-tobacco crusade?

WRITE ABOUT IT

The Tobacco Industry

Write a composition on one of the following topics.

a) How much influence does tobacco advertising have on teen smoking?

or

b) Discuss how tobacco companies could and should be regulated.

Compound Adjectives

Adjectives are always singular in English.

> We have an **old** car. We have two **old** cars.

They may have two parts joined by a hyphen.

> I have a **ten-dollar** bill. It was a **record-breaking** crowd.

A   Match the compound adjectives with the nouns they describe.

1.	a middle-aged	a)	smoke
2.	an anti-smoking	b)	race
3.	an eight-year-old	c)	activists
4.	a name-brand	d)	campaign
5.	second-hand	e)	product
6.	a quick-acting	f)	person
7.	a high-speed	g)	pain reliever
8.	anti-tobacco	h)	vest
9.	a low-fat	i)	boy
10.	a bullet-proof	j)	granola bar

B   Make compound adjectives from the information below.

> a car that looks good   a **good-looking** car

1. a book that sells more than any other book
2. a man who has a strange appearance
3. a river in which the water flows fast
4. a machine with multiple purposes
5. a flower that smells sweet
6. a bottle that resists being tampered with
7. a politician who is hungry for power
8. a fish that lives in salt water

9. a fruit with a sour taste

10. a word with many syllables

11. a product that has been test marketed

12. a plane that is flying low

13. a person who is weary of the world

14. a country torn apart by war

15. a con artist who talks fast

AT LAST

Now that you have finished the unit, go back to the activity "What's Your Take On This?" and discuss the questions again.

WHOM?

havoc (havvik)

barely = means just finish .

Where Should the Money Come From?

Work in a group to discuss the questions below.

1. Should sports events or cultural festivals (such as the Montreal Jazz Festival) get funding from the tobacco industry?

2. Should drug stores be allowed to sell tobacco products?

3. Is it ethical for medical associations to endorse specific brands of drugs in exchange for funding?

4. Is it appropriate for drug companies to fund research into diseases and their treatment of diseases?

5. Should doctors or medical students get free trips, dinners, conferences, and other perks from drug companies?

RAISING FUNDS

Medical research is very costly. Sports and cultural events are suffering from cuts to government funding. Given these facts, how do you think foundations, charities, and organizing committees should raise funds?

 A Discuss these ideas. Which of the following methods do you think are appropriate?

1. try to get government grants

2. solicit money from individuals (e.g., in donations or wills)

3. hold public subscription campaigns

4. endorse products in harmony with their aims (e.g., running shoes)

5. accept money in exchange for endorsements of any product

B What are the advantages and disadvantages of the various solutions above?

CORPORATE DONATIONS

 A Watch the video. Summarize the information by answering the questions below.

1. Describe traditional ways for charitable foundations to raise money.

2. Why are businesses being approached for donations?

3. Explain the term "strategic philanthropy."

4. Give examples of strategic philanthropy.

5. How do companies benefit from strategic partnerships?

 B Give your opinion of the issues raised in the video. Discuss the questions.

1. How do you feel about sources of funding for charity, based on statistics from the video?

2. How would you decide what causes or charities you would contribute to?

"Must" for Deduction

One use of the modal auxiliary **must** is to express deductions.

1. To express deductions in present time, use **must** before the bare infinitive.

> John has to make a big decision. He **must feel** nervous.

2. To express deductions in past time, use **must** + the base form of **have** + the past participle of the main verb.

> Many foundations needed to raise money. They **must have been** desperate.

A Express deductions based on the information given.

> Janet is waiting at the microphone.
> She **must have** something to say.

1. Susan just took two aspirins.

2. Min Hee is yawning a lot.

3. Marco has big muscles.

4. The dog is sitting near the door.

5. They are looking at a city map.

6. Junko is coughing a lot.

7. Gaby is putting on sandals.

8. Something is making me sneeze.

9. The government is increasing taxes.

10. Max is pouring a large glass of water.

CANADIAN CAPSULES

The largest fundraising organization in Canada is the United Way of Greater Toronto. It has about 60 000 volunteers and raises approximately $50 million annually.

B   Look at the pictures and write deductions in past time.

WHO DO YOU TRUST?

If you needed advice related to your health or lifestyle, what would be a good source of information?

A   Work in a group and put the following in order. Rank the most trustworthy as 1.

- TV advertisers
- the Canadian Heart Fund
- the Canadian Medical Association
- a tennis or swimming champion
- the Canadian Dental Association
- your family doctor
- a government information brochure
- a friend with the same problem as you

B   What are the advantages and disadvantages of the various solutions above?

UNDER ATTACK

A   Skim the article to match the two parts of each sentence.

1. Paul Root Wolpe feels that
2. Marketers are seeking
3. Medical organizations will soon
4. The Arthritis Foundation is ready to
5. The Stroh Brewing Company got more sales by
6. SmithKlein Beecham PLC will pay for
7. The American Cancer Society would accept funds from
8. The American Heart Association endorses

---

a) promote all kinds of products for profit.

b) companies that support their mission.

c) credibility through association.

d) donating to cultural causes.

e) low-fat, low-cholesterol foods.

f) the American Cancer Society will hurt its credibility by endorsing certain products.

g) a partnership with the Cancer Society.

h) put its logo on painkillers.

Under Attack

Steve Sakson

1. The American Cancer Society is selling its name to two corporate giants, offering exclusive endorsements to NicoDerm anti-smoking patches and Florida orange juice for at least $4 million. Ethical watchdogs denounced the deals announced yesterday, saying the society might seriously hurt its credibility. "If they want to endorse products, they should do it in the spirit of an educational agency, not as a paid shill," said Paul Root Wolpe of the Center for Bioethics at the University of Pennsylvania.

2. The deals, part of a rising trend of partnerships between non-profit groups and companies, will provide the society with cash to boost its cancer-fighting programs and meet a $427 million annual budget at a time when donations are stagnant. They also give the marketers of these products instant credibility through their association with one of America's most respected health groups.

3. But if the trend accelerates, Wolpe predicted, medical organizations will some day be endorsing everything from chewing gum to sneakers. "We're going to end up with the health equivalent of the Olympics," he said, adding, "On the other hand I deeply understand the temptation." That temptation snagged its last big medical association two years ago when the Arthritis Foundation signed a $1 million deal with the makers of Tylenol to sell painkillers with the foundation name on the boxes.

4. Corporate executives call it cause-related marketing, something that got their attention in a big way in the 1980s when surveys showed most people would switch brands—and even pay more—if the companies making those products advocated causes with which they agree. American Express Corp., the Stroh Brewing Co., and others accelerated the trend when they racked up higher sales by donating a portion of profits to the restoration of the Statue of Liberty and Ellis Island, said Daniel Borochoff, president of the watchdog American Institute of Philanthropy in St. Louis.

5. Yesterday's deal was announced in conjunction with the introduction of NicoDerm CQ, the second nicotine patch to be made available as an over-the-counter drug in the US. SmithKlein Beecham PLC, the British-based drug manufacturer, will pay the Cancer Society at least $1 million per year in sales royalties for three years. In exchange, the society's logo will appear on NicoDerm CQ boxes and advertising, along with a reference to the two as partners in promoting smoking cessation.

6. In a similar deal, the Florida citrus marketer's association agreed to pay the society at least $1 million for one year. "After very serious consideration and review, we determined that companies that are producing products that support the missions or programs of the American Cancer Society would be acceptable business partners for us," said society spokesperson Elizabeth Bridgers.

7. Nicotine patches, worn on the arm, gradually ooze nicotine into the smoker's body, helping stave off the craving for cigarettes. Sales were mediocre as prescription-only products, but the patches are now expected to generate hundreds of millions of dollars in over-the-counter sales, with millions of smokers trying to quit. The competition is expected to be stiff, and American airwaves, magazines and newspapers are going to be filled with multimillion-dollar advertising campaigns.

8. As for orange juice, while there is no direct proof it prevents cancer, Bridgers said drinking it can be part of a healthy diet and "eating healthy is one of the major preventive measures against cancer." Some groups endorse products without making exclusive deals. The American Dental Association puts its seal of approval on toothpaste with fluoride and the American Heart Association endorses low-fat, low-cholesterol foods.

9. Ethicists say the American Cancer Society takes a risk with its deal with SmithKlein because other nicotine patches might come along that work better. Just last week, research partly funded by the society showed that combining patches with the drug mecamylamine enhances effectiveness. They're saying, "OK, we're no longer a place to go for counsel and advice on nicotine patches because we've been bought by this company on this one issue," Borochoff said.

B Read the article and answer the questions.

1. Why were many people upset at the American Cancer Society's endorsement of the NicoDerm patch?

2. How will both parties benefit in the partnership between the Cancer Society and the product marketers?

3. What is cause-related marketing?

4. Why is cause-related marketing so attractive to companies?

5. How have American Express Corp. and other companies profited from the trend to cause-related marketing?

6. What rationale does the American Cancer Society spokesperson give for endorsing Florida orange juice?

7. Why are anti-smoking patches expected to generate millions of dollars of sales even though they were not very successful in the past?

8. What kinds of deals are made that do not endorse specific products?

9. What is the risk that ethicists associate with the American Cancer Society's endorsement of the NicoDerm patch?

10. What warning does Borochoff give about the NicoDerm patch deal?

CANADIAN CAPSULES The annual Manulife Ride for Heart fundraiser, held in Toronto, is one of Canada's largest cycling events. Held on a Sunday in June, it attracts about 8000 participants every year.

C   Use the text to help you complete this puzzle.

Across

1. tough (paragraph 7)

5. promotes (paragraph 8)

6. connection (paragraph 5)

9. company (paragraph 1)

10. promoted (paragraph 4)

12. so-so (paragraph 7)

13. money (paragraph 2)

14. caught (paragraph 3)

15. increases (paragraph 9)

17. spoke against (paragraph 1)

18. goals (paragraph 6)

Down

2. paid for (paragraph 9)

3. cooperations (paragraph 2)

4. repair (paragraph 4)

7. picks up speed (paragraph 3)

8. symbol (paragraph 5)

11. arrangement (paragraph 3)

14. at a standstill (paragraph 2)

16. change (paragraph 4)

LANGUAGE AND CULTURE

Find the expressions below in the article "Under Attack." Choose the best definitions.

1. "ethical watchdogs"
   a) police officers
   b) moral advisors

2. "non-profit groups"
   a) badly-run companies
   b) foundations

3. "the health equivalent of the Olympics"
   a) heavily dependent on corporate sponsorship
   b) related to popular sporting events

4. "Ellis Island"
   a) an amusement park near New York City
   b) a centre for processing immigrants

5. "over-the-counter drugs"
   a) non-prescription medications
   b) easy to find drugs

6. "sales royalties"
   a) a percentage of sales
   b) royal endorsement of products

7. "a spokesperson"
   a) a representative of an organization
   b) a news reporter on television

8. "American airwaves"
   a) overseas publicity campaigns
   b) radio and television programs

9. "a preventative measure"
   a) a way to avoid something undesirable
   b) a way to fix a problem that arises

CANADIAN CAPSULES

M.A.C., a cosmetics company that started in Canada, regularly donates a percentage of its profits to AIDS research.

WRITE ABOUT IT

Sponsorship

Write a composition on one of the themes below, giving your view on the controversial topic of the endorsement of various products by charitable foundations.

a) Selling sponsorship to business in exchange for charitable contributions is defensible in certain circumstances.

   or

b) Entering into sponsorship agreements with corporations compromises the ethical positions of charitable foundations.

PERFECT YOUR ENGLISH

Duplicates

Babies' first sounds are usually repetitions such as "mama," "baba," and "papa." It isn't surprising that so many languages uses variations of these sounds to describe the most important people in a child's life—his or her parents. Later in life, repetitive words may reflect human love of symmetry. After all, we have two arms, two legs, two eyes, two ears, and so on.

The English language has many examples of duplicate, or near-duplicate words. Some of them are used by children. Others sound as if they should be. Still others have a lyrical quality and sound as if they belong in poetry.

    A   Work with a partner to say these duplicate words and match them to the meanings on the next page.

1. mumbo-jumbo
2. pitter-patter
3. a walkie-talkie
4. a fender-bender
5. hanky-panky
6. hush-hush
7. riff-raff
8. a fuddy-duddy
9. super-duper
10. hocus-pocus
11. a bon-bon
12. beriberi
13. a murmur
14. a boo-boo
15. gaga

a) a very proper, old-fashioned personality

b) a tropical disease

c) a French candy

d) something without much worth

e) something secret

f) something morally dubious

g) foolish, crazy

h) a small injury

i) a quiet sound

j) a minor car accident

k) the sound of little feet or raindrops

l) a portable communication device

m) magic

n) superb, stupendous

o) nonsense

B Can you add to the list of double words in English? Do you know of similar words in other languages? Share them with your class.

AT LAST

Now that you have finished the unit, go back to the activity "What's Your Take On This?" and discuss the questions again.

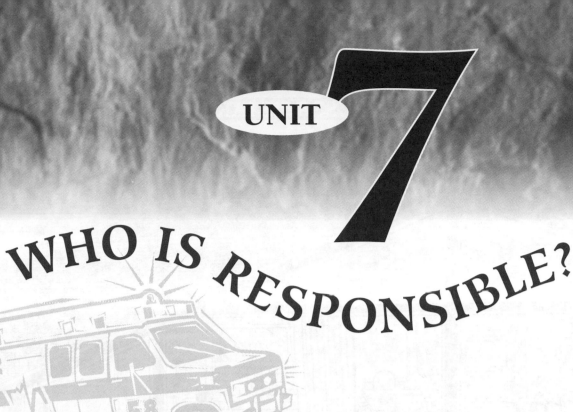

WHO IS RESPONSIBLE?

WHAT'S YOUR TAKE ON THIS?

Accepting Responsibility

Work in groups to discuss the questions.

1. What are some disasters that can be caused by human carelessness?

2. If someone deliberately sets fire to a building, he or she will be charged with arson. What happens if someone sets fire to a building by smoking in bed and falling asleep?

3. What role do you think government should play in promoting safety by methods such as enforcing car safety inspections and smoking regulations or instituting fire-prevention campaigns?

4. Do you think people in apartment buildings should be required to have smoke detectors?

5. Should there be a punishment for carelessness that causes accidents?

CARELESS MISTAKES

  A Work with a partner. Look at the picture of the house. List the safety mistakes in each room.

B Put the safety mistakes you identified in the picture into categories.

Electrical problems	Poisons	Physical injury	Special danger to children	Other

 C Discuss these questions in a group.

1. What could happen as a result of each safety mistake?

2. Who is responsible for each of the situations?

3. What could be done to prevent an accident from happening in each of the situations?

YOU DECIDE

 Read about these two cases and answer the questions that follow.

Case 1

A man plugs a few space heaters into an electric socket and then heads out to the movies. While he's gone, the circuit blows. Electric sparks spray onto his rug. The room begins to fill with smoke. Right about now, the smoke alarm should go off. But the man dismantled the fire alarm last time dinner burned. The fire breaks out and spreads for an hour or so before anyone detects it. Adjacent apartments are destroyed, someone jumps to his death, and an old woman perishes of smoke inhalation.

Case 2

Someone drinks too much at a party and then insists on driving home. He can't control the car properly and weaves all over the road, causing other cars to swerve out of the way. As he runs a red light and drives up on the sidewalk, the police stop him and give him a breathalyser test. They find he is over the legal limit and when they check the computer in the patrol car, they discover that he has had his driver's licence suspended for drunk driving in the past. Nobody has been hurt, however, and no property has been damaged.

Questions

1. What are some similarities and differences between these two cases?

2. Which case is more serious and why?

3. What do you think would be the legal consequences of each of these cases in North America?

4. What would happen in other countries in such cases?

5. What punishment, if any, do you think is appropriate in each of the cases?

THE ALL-AMERICAN FIRE TRAP

A   Work in a group. Look at the statements below and decide whether they are **true** or **false**.

1. More fires occur annually in New York City than in all of Japan.

2. Despite the fact that many houses in Japan are built from wood and paper, house fires are not a big problem there.

3. An increase in the use of smoke alarms has decreased the danger of fires in American cities.

4. The sound of fire engine sirens is a feature of big cities all over the world.

5. Some countries imprison people who are responsible for starting fires by careless smoking.

6. Arson is a common crime in European countries such as France and Switzerland.

7. More than 5000 people die in fires in the United States every year.

8. A drunk driver in the United States can go to jail only if he is responsible for killing or injuring other people.

9. In North America, firefighters are considered heroes.

10. Most fires in North America are the result of carelessness and indifference to risk.

Over 10 percent of fatal traffic accidents are caused by drivers who fall asleep at the wheel.

B Scan the article quickly to check your answers to the questions.

The All-American Fire Trap

Jon McMillan

1. North Americans start 40 times as many fires per capita as the Japanese do. New York city alone has more fires each year than all of Japan, where 120 million people live in tightly-packed wood houses with paper walls and reed-covered floors. Despite an increasing use of sprinklers and smoke alarms, the US has tallied the worst fire death rate in the industrialized world for decades.

2. How come fire trucks careen up my stretch of Sixth Avenue all day and all night long? Maybe some people get used to New York's ubiquitous fire engines and their head-splitting honks. I might have, if I hadn't lived in Paris for a year. I don't remember ever hearing or seeing a fire truck the entire time I was there.

3. Americans have the world's most advanced fire-protection technology and best-trained firemen. Yet these advantages seem to contribute to our indifference about letting fires start. We permit millions of fires that other countries don't.

4. Surely, this is because in the US fires are not really considered anyone's fault. They are usually accidental. When someone loses track of his cigarette and sets his home ablaze (the No. 1 cause of fires) he isn't thrown in jail because, of course, he didn't set the fire on purpose.

5. Japan and several European countries impose severe penalties no matter how unintentional a fire is. Someone irresponsibly allowed the circumstances to develop that caused a fire; that someone can go right to jail. The crime is called "grave negligence," and the punishment can be life imprisonment. Strict penalties for careless fires deter you from smoking in bed, leaving pans on the stove, or overloading the electric circuitry. And that's just the beginning.

6. In Germany, you will be personally liable for the damage done to anyone else's property like the house next door or the apartment upstairs. If someone dies, it's manslaughter.

7. In France you won't get much help from insurance companies; their policies are carefully designed to make you poorer after any fire even if it's not your fault. Switzerland lets you use insurance proceeds only to rebuild exactly the same structure on the same lot; you won't see any cash and that pretty much eliminates arson.

8. But in the US, suppose the fellow in the apartment downstairs plugs a few space heaters into an electric socket and then heads out to the movies. While he's gone, the circuit blows. Electric sparks spray onto his rug. The room begins to fill with smoke. Right about now, the smoke alarm should go off. But not only has your neighbour let the batteries in his alarm run

➡

down, he disengaged the whole thing last time dinner burned. The fire breaks out and spreads for an hour or so before anyone detects it.

9. What happens to this guy if adjacent apartments are destroyed, someone jumps to his death, and an old woman perishes of smoke inhalation? Nothing. Legally, its just an accident. This kind of carelessness adds up to about 5000 deaths, two million severe burn injuries (which are very costly to treat), and $8 billion in property losses a year.

10. If you drink and drive in the US, you can go to prison, even if no one is harmed. If you drink and start a fire—half of all fires involve alcohol—it's an accident, even if you kill your wife and kids and burn down the whole block.

11. Why are Americans so indifferent to preventing fires? Those who study fire safety in other countries say the reasons are cultural. In the US, fire codes and regulations are concentrated on public buildings and not on individual homes and apartments, where 80 percent of fire-related deaths occur. We are reluctant to regulate what people do in the privacy of their homes even though what they do can harm others.

12. We also don't teach enough fire safety. Japan, by contrast, incorporates it into class work in school. London's fire department spends $1 million a year just on TV commercials. Entire neighbourhoods in South Korea have fire drills; every apartment in Seoul has a fire marshal. Meanwhile, in North America, firemen seem to occupy a heroic spot in the culture. This leads to a national focus on fire fighting rather than fire prevention.

13. Whatever the reasons for American pyromania, Europe and Asia offer proof that most fires in North America are caused by sheer indifference to the risk. We should criminalize such reckless behaviour, just as we did drunk driving. The fellow downstairs should probably spend a year in jail.

C   Answer the questions.

1. What is surprising about the information at the end of the first paragraph?

2. What surprising contrast does the author mention in the second paragraph?

3. What contradiction is identified in paragraph 3?

4. What explanation is offered for this contradiction in paragraph 4?

5. What reasoning leads some European countries to impose strict penalties in the case of "accidental" fires?

6. What is the German attitude towards fire damage?

7. Give statistics on the outcome of fires in the United States every year.

8. Contrast the penalties for drinking and driving with those for accidentally starting a fire in the United States.

9. What explains American indifference to fire prevention?

10. How does the public see firefighters in North America?

11. What does the author suggest is the answer to the high rate of fires in North America?

D Look at the article to find synonyms for the following words.

paragraph 1: counted

paragraph 2: ever-present

paragraph 3: allow

paragraph 4: forget

paragraph 5: carelessness

paragraph 6: responsible

paragraph 7: compensation

paragraph 8: unplugged

paragraph 9: (apartment) next door

paragraph 10: jail

paragraph 11: injure

paragraph 12: ads

paragraph 13: complete

GRAMMAR FOCUS · "Hope" and "Wish"

Both **hope** and **wish** are used to describe situations you would like to happen in future. **Hope** describes future possibilities. **Wish** describes hypothetical (unreal) situations.

"Hope"

Hope describes things that are possible. You don't know, however, whether they will happen or not.

| I hope we arrive on time. |

CANADIAN CAPSULES Car thieves in Canada have an easy time. Over 40 percent of cars stolen have been left running, have had keys in the ignition, or have been left unlocked.

A   Match the situations with the responses below.

1. That building on the corner is on fire.

2. Some people seem to be injured.

3. There are too many appliances plugged into the same outlet.

4. A young child is climbing out of her crib.

5. A pipe in the basement is leaking.

6. The man who lives upstairs smokes in bed.

7. That person plans to drive his car after drinking wine with dinner.

8. No one in that car is wearing a seat belt.

9. The traffic is really heavy on the way to the airport.

10. A woman just slipped on the icy sidewalk.

---

a) I hope he doesn't hit someone.

b) I hope we get there on time.

c) I hope she didn't break her leg.

d) I hope the plumber gets here soon.

e) I hope the ambulance arrives soon.

f) I hope everyone is outside.

g) I hope it doesn't start a fire.

h) I hope she doesn't fall and get hurt.

i) I hope he doesn't fall asleep with a cigarette in his hand.

j) I hope they don't get into an accident.

B   First, match the questions with the pictures on page 85. Then answer the questions with **I hope so** or **I hope not**.

1. Is he going to pass his exams?

2. Is he going to hit the tricycle?

3. Is she going to fall?

4. Will she be all right?

5. Is she going to drop anything?

6. Is it going to be a nice day?

7. Will they be able to put it out?

8. Will the cat escape?

9. Will she like her new cut?

"Wish"

Wish describes unreal situations. Use **I wish** for things you would like to happen (even though they are not real possibilities). **I wish** is followed by a noun clause (either with or without **that**).

> I wish (that) I could fly.

The verb in the clause after **wish** is expressed in an earlier time than the situation that led to the wish.

> Present: I don't know what to do.
>
> Past: I wish I did (know).

> Present: We can't do anything about it.
>
> Past: We wish we could (do something).

> Past: She arrived at the office late.
>
> Past perfect: She wishes she had arrived earlier.

> Present perfect: The car hasn't passed a safety inspection.
>
> Past perfect: I wish it had (passed one).

A   Complete the sentences with the correct form of the verb.

1. We don't have time to finish.

   I wish we _____.

2. They can't get through the traffic.

   They wish they _____.

3. She didn't have anything to eat at noon.

   She wishes she _____.

4. It hasn't rained for a month.

   The farmer wishes it _____.

5. I don't have time to watch TV often.

   I wish I _____.

6. I can't remember how to get there.

   I wish I _____.

7. You don't agree with me.

   I wish you _____.

8. He fell asleep at the wheel.

He wishes he _____.

9 I didn't wear a raincoat.

I wish I _____.

10. It gets dark early all winter.

I wish it _____.

ON THE DEFENCE

Read about these cases and then discuss them in a group.

Situation

A man asks a lawyer to defend him in court. Before taking the case, the lawyer asks the man what crime he is accused of. The man answers that his wife's body was found in the garage of their home. She had been beaten to death. He has been charged with murder and is out on bail.

As the lawyer, you have to decide whether to take the case or not. As you question the man about the crime, you get the following information. Look at each case and decide how comfortable you would feel defending the accused in each one.

Case 1

The accused has lived in the community for 15 years and has a reputation as a good husband and father. On the night of the crime he was driving back from another city where he had been on business. On the way, he was involved in a traffic accident. At the scene of the murder, the police found no signs of a break-in. They had been called by a neighbour who said she had gone to return a lawnmower she had borrowed from the murdered woman, found the garage door ajar, and seen the woman's body in a pool of blood. The accused is distraught about the death of his wife and devastated that anyone would imagine him responsible.

Case 2

The man has lived in the neighbourhood for two years. The police have frequently been called to investigate reports of domestic violence. The wife mentioned to friends that she was afraid of her husband because he had a violent temper, but she refused to make a police report. The night of the murder the husband claimed to have been in a bar but he is unable to remember the name of the bar because he was too drunk. The body was discovered by the couple next door who heard screams and went to see if they could help. The man is angry with the police, claiming he has been framed just because he has a previous record for assault.

TAKING THE CASE

  LISTENING ACTIVITY **4** *Interview with Raphael Schacter, Criminal Lawyer*

Listen to the interview. Then discuss the questions in a group.

1. What is the question the interviewer asks Raphael Schacter?

2. What does Schacter's acquaintance from Oxford feel about the same question?

3. How does Schacter describe the "adversarial system"?

4. What are some rights the accused has under the system?

5. What theoretical idea underlies this system?

6. How does Schacter explain that he could hypothetically either defend or prosecute the same person?

7. What is Schacter's reason for wanting to know whether a person he is defending is really guilty?

8. What strategic reason could make it inadvisable for an innocent person to testify on his or her own behalf?

LANGUAGE AND CULTURE

 Listen again for these expressions. When the teacher stops the tape, explain what they mean.

1. jumping the gun

2. to pull the trigger

3. the criminal **walked**

4. worked **both sides of the street**

5. a knock on the door at four o'clock in the morning

6. the devil I'm dealing with

7. take the stand

8. He's done it again.

PERFECT YOUR ENGLISH

Oxymorons

Oxymorons are terms that contradict themselves. The word "oxymoron" comes from the Greek words "oxy," which means "sharp" and "moros" which means "foolish."

The expression "jumbo shrimp" is an oxymoron because shrimp are usually small, and the word "shrimp" is used in many cases to mean "small," while "jumbo" means big.

Oxymorons can be used to convey irony, or just for fun. Look out for oxymorons in advertisements or TV commercials.

  A Look at the list below and discuss the contradiction in each expression.

1. a minor catastrophe
2. white chocolate
3. hot ice
4. bittersweet
5. a baby grand (piano)
6. sugar-free candy
7. a mobile home
8. a fair tax
9. a point in time
10. awfully good
11. educational television
12. military intelligence
13. nightly specials
14. a death benefit
15. a family vacation

B Which of the expressions above could be used ironically? What point of view makes them ironic?

  C Work in groups. Think of some other oxymorons you have heard. Try to come up with some new oxymorons. Share them with the group.

AT LAST

 Now that you have finished the unit, go back to the activity "What's Your Take On This?" and discuss the questions again.

YOUR GRANDMOTHER'S GENES

	YES	NO
Heart Disease	✓	
Arthritis	✓	
Cancer		✓
Diabetes		✓
Stress	✓	
Smoker		✓
Allergies		✓
Drug Abuse		✓
Alcohol Abuse		✓

WHAT'S YOUR TAKE ON THIS?

Your Medical History

Work in a group to discuss these questions.

1. Do you think there are circumstances in which an employer would need and should have access to the medical history of an employee?

2. Should a company have the right to refuse employment to someone based on his or her medical condition or medical history?

3. How much of a person's health profile is accounted for by environmental factors and how much by heredity?

4. If there is a hereditary disease in a person's family, does that mean the person will inherit it?

5. Should employers have access to genetic information about their employees' health before hiring them?

6. Should the government act to protect the privacy of people's medical histories?

THE HUMAN GENOME PROJECT

 Chose the best words to complete these paragraphs.

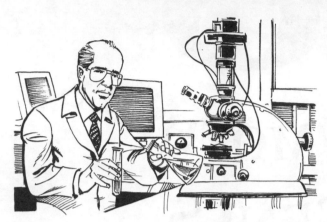

One of the great scientific accomplishments of the turn of the century is currently being (**1.** fund, funded, funding) by the US government. This project is on a par with nuclear physics (**2.** as, like, same) a revolutionary scientific discovery. Specifically, the project (**3.** shoots, tries, aims) at mapping the human genome, the genetic material that makes us what we are. This massive undertaking seeks (**4.** decipher, deciphering, to decipher) the 60 000 to 100 000 genes in the human genome. It has the potential to (**5.** give, open, provide) scientists with a window on the mysteries of human inheritance and to uncover cures for many diseases that seem to run in families.

Yet, for all (**6.** it's, its, is) enormous potential, the Human Genome Project is not without controversy. With new genes (**7.** are, being, have) found on a daily basis, the teaching of biology is being transformed. Suddenly, modern genetics has a relevance for everyday concerns (**8.** who, what, that) were unimaginable 20 years (**9.** ago, before, past). Indeed, a portion of the funding for the Human Genome Project is set aside for (**10.** moral, practical, ethical) questions. Yet already many Americans are being asked to undergo genetic tests for insurance or employment applications.

SCIENCE AND US

Work in a group. Discuss the questions.

1. Did you inherit any physical characteristics from your parents?

2. If you could change something about yourself, what would it be?

3. Is there anyone in your family who has the same temperament as you do?

4. What physical or emotional traits would you like to pass on to your children?

5. To what extent do you think heredity plays a role in the kinds of people we become?

6. How much influence does environment have on how people turn out?

WRITE ABOUT IT

Who You Are

Write a composition describing some of the factors that you think have contributed to who you are today.

GENETIC JOB LOSS

A Skim the article to find the following information:

1. why an employer would fire someone who had done nothing wrong
2. what trend is beginning in the United States and may spread
3. the number of US companies using genetic screening in the 1980s
4. two reasons large firms might examine their employees' genes
5. what steps companies might take if they can't afford genetic tests
6. what some leading geneticists are calling for
7. what Professor Davies predicts for the future
8. one of the few circumstances in which Bodmer would accept the use of genetic tests in employment
9. what Simon Barrow thinks would be of interest to recruiters
10. how genetic discrimination could lead to racial discrimination

Genetic Job Loss

Valida Starcevich

Discrimination is growing as recruiters check our DNA

1. Imagine you are called in by your boss—and fired. You are told you have done nothing wrong—but your genes show a predisposition to a certain kind of illness. There is only a 20 percent probability that you will contract this illness, but it is cheaper for your employer to take on someone with a cleaner record.

2. This does not happen everywhere but—if the world follows the Americans—it is probably just a matter of time. In the United States, you can be fired because of the illnesses of your ancestors. Employees are often required to take genetic tests that can reveal a predisposition to illness. People with a defective gene may never be sick, but they may be fired—just in case. A sick employee is an expensive burden many companies do not want to carry.

3. In the mid-1980s several research studies in the US predicted that competitive pressure would soon lead to widespread genetic screening for recruitment. Only half a dozen leading corporations were using genetic tests then, but another 60 were considering using them.

4. The US Equal Opportunity Commission estimates that 5 percent of large American firms examine their employees' genes. Pressure from the competition and health-insurance costs—which are often paid by an employer—destroy the employment prospects for many people carrying a defective gene.

➡

Companies check histories

5. Companies that cannot afford the expense of tests make do by investigating the family medical history. A woman in her twenties, fired because her mother suffered from Huntington's chorea, made the headlines; but she is not the only one. In the US labour market, genetic discrimination is growing faster than the pressure of campaigners to introduce protective legislation.

6. Huntington's chorea is a rare hereditary brain disorder. It usually develops in people in their thirties and may progress for 10 to 20 years until the patient dies. A woman has a 50-50 chance of inheriting her mother's condition.

7. As the need for private insurance grows in many countries, so does the power of insurance companies on employers. Leading geneticists are calling for laws to ban abuses of genetic tests by employers and insurance companies.

Common disorders detectable

8. It is now possible to identify some single-gene defects, such as muscular dystrophy and cystic fibrosis, and to screen for susceptibility to some cancers. Professor Kay Davies, of Oxford University in England, believes that in the next century it will be possible to calculate an individual's susceptibility to far more common disorders such as diabetes, ischemic heart disease, asthma, and rheumatoid arthritis.

9. Sir Walter Bodmer, director of the Imperial Cancer Research Fund, would exclude the use of genetic tests in employment. "Safety risks can justify testing pilots for colour blindness, but the cases when predisposition to certain diseases should be relevant for an employer are extremely rare," he says. His worries multiplied after talking to the London Recruitment Society: recruiters do not seem to share the geneticist's anxiety.

10. Simon Barrow, chair of the society, says, "If there was a way of detecting behavioural genes that determine consistency, resoluteness or stamina, recruiters would be interested. It is clear that the time will come when it will be possible to talk about behaviour genes just as it is now possible to talk about physical ones."

11. Barrow thinks that the fact someone might develop an illness in 30 years' time should not be of interest to recruiters. Medical experts agree that genes do not determine our health, talents, or behavioural traits and that their contribution is as relevant as a range of environmental factors. Our health is the result of various influences.

12. A drop of blood is easy to get and even easier to analyze. Some defective genes are more frequent in particular ethnic groups: genetic discrimination could become another kind of racial discrimination.

B   Look in the article to find nouns and adjectives that are made from these root words. The paragraph numbers are beside the words. In some cases, more than one word may be derived from the root.

Make a list of the words you find.

1. ill (1)
2. probable (1)
3. gene (2)
4. defect (2)
5. expense (3)
6. compete (3)
7. recruit (3)
8. employ (4)
9. discriminate (5)
10. protect (5)
11. heir (6)
12. insure (7)
13. muscle (8)
14. empire (9)
15. blind (9)
16. behave (10)
17. resolute (10)
18. environment (11)

LANGUAGE AND CULTURE

 Discuss these expressions. What do they refer to?

1. a sick employee is an **expensive burden**
2. a **leading** corporation
3. an **Equal Opportunity** Commission
4. made the **headlines**
5. **protective** legislation
6. a **50-50** chance
7. **private** insurance
8. particular **ethnic** groups
9. **racial** discrimination

 **CANADIAN CAPSULES**

It is estimated that in fewer than ten years, scientists will have deciphered the 60 000 to 100 000 genes in the human genome.

Causative Verb Phrases

In a causative statement, the verb **have** indicates that two people (a causer and a doer) are responsible for the action described in the statement. The causer either can't or doesn't want to do the action, and therefore causes someone else to do it.

Causative with "Have": Causer and Doer Mentioned

Use **have** to suggest the causative, and the base form of the main verb.

> The **employer** has the **personnel department** screen all the applicants.
>   causer   doer

A Complete the sentences by choosing a doer from the list below.

the mechanic   his accountant   all employees   the company his doctor   applicants   the patients   the clinic   her secretary a medical journal

1. Most of the employees are having _____ deposit their pay cheques directly in their bank accounts.

2. George is having _____ prepare his income tax returns early this year.

3. The receptionist usually has _____ send in application forms before they come for their interviews.

4. The director had _____ phone the candidates to give them appointments for their interviews.

5. The sales rep had _____ check the pressure in his tires before he went on the road.

6. One company has _____ submit complete medical reports before it hires them permanently.

7. Marshall has _____ check his blood pressure regularly since his heart attack.

8. The researcher is having _____ publish the findings of his study on hereditary illness.

9. The nurse in the clinic had _____ get undressed before they were examined by the doctor.

10. The director of personnel had _____ send all the medical reports to his office as confidential documents.

Causative with "Have": Only the Causer Mentioned

The grammatical form of the sentence indicates that the action was caused by one person and done by another person. Use **have** to suggest the causative. Omit mention of the doer. Use the past participle for the main verb.

> The **director of personnel** had **all candidates examined** medically.
>   causer   object   action

 Rewrite the sentences, omitting mention of the doer and making the necessary grammatical changes.

> The candidate will have a photographer take her picture.
> **The candidate will have her picture taken.**

1. Mario has the doctor check his blood pressure once a month.

2. Employers are having catering services bring coffee to their employees.

3. My neighbour is having a mechanic check her brakes for problems.

4. Some offices have employees recycle waste paper these days.

5. Some companies have doctors screen their employees for genetic defects.

6. Janet had the telephone company disconnect her service while she was away.

7. Walter had someone from the repair department fix his computer.

8. The boss has someone clean his office every weekend.

9. Francine had the lab forward the results of her blood test to the company doctor.

10. The union had its lawyer take the company to court over genetic testing.

Note: In a causative statement, the verb **have** can be replaced with the verb **get,** with a small difference in form. With **get,** the main verb is expressed as the infinitive.

> The doctor **got** the lab **to send** him the reports.

YOUR GENETIC PROFILE

  VIDEO ACTIVITY 4

A   Watch the video. Summarize the information by discussing the following:

1.   why insurance companies have a stake in people's genetic forecasts

2.   the goal of the genome project

3.   why there is such excitement about what genetic researchers are finding

4.   the privacy issue raised in the video

5.   Dr. Sandy Lauden's position on insurance companies' right to information

6.   some reasons why researchers argue for the importance of privacy in access to genetic information

7.   how the three people in the video were discriminated against by insurance companies

8.   What are Dr. Hayden's fears about giving the results of tests for Huntington's chorea to insurance companies?

 B   Give your opinion of the issues raised in the video. Discuss these questions.

1.   What are the potential benefits of genetic testing?

2.   What are the potential drawbacks?

3.   Would you want to undergo genetic testing?

4.   Do you find the insurance companies' position reasonable?

WRITE ABOUT IT

Genetic Testing

 Genetic testing is becoming a controversial issue. Some people are concerned about the uses to which the information from genetic tests can be put. Others emphasize the benefits of finding cures for diseases that are currently incurable. What is your feeling about genetic testing? Write about one of the following topics.

a)   Should genetic testing continue?

or

b)   Who should have access to your genetic information?

PERFECT YOUR ENGLISH

Words to Soften and Distract

Someone once described Canadians as more modest and conservative than Americans.

One characteristic of Canadian speech patterns is the tendency to soften requests with, "I was wondering if you could…." We also lighten the force of our words with phrases such as, "I suppose…," "I guess…," or "It seems to me that…."

We may also soften our words by adding such expressions as "basically," "roughly," or "to some extent." We solicit agreement by ending sentences with phrases such as "Don't you agree?", "Right?" or the famous Canadian tag ending "eh?" as in the sentence, "It's really cold today, eh?"

One popular interjection Canadians use a lot is "like." Look at the examples of how "like" may be used.

- to suggest similarity: It's hot, like in the tropics.

- to give approximations: It took us, like, six hours to get here.

- to give reinforcement: There were, like, 20 centimetres of snow last night!

- to show excitement: We, like, won three games in a row!

- to moderate a comment: She's, like, amazing.

Teenagers are the greatest users of "like". Here is an example of what you might hear in a typical teenage conversation.

"We went to the game, like, and it was, like, great! Our team, like, won, and it was, like, fantastic!"

A Work in a group and see if you can think of, like, other softeners and interjections you have heard used in conversation.

B Write a "Canadian" dialogue using softeners and interjections.

AT LAST

Now that you have finished the unit, go back to the activity "What's Your Take On This?" and discuss the questions again.

MINDING EACH OTHER'S BUSINESS

WHAT'S YOUR TAKE ON THIS?

What's On the Tube?

A   Discuss these questions in a group.

1.   Have you ever watched talk shows on television?

2.   Which ones do you think are most interesting?

3.   Have you seen anything that surprised you on these shows?

4.   Do you think talk shows give a realistic portrait of North American life?

5.   What kind of information or subject matter do you think should be banned?

6.   Whose responsibility is it to police the content of talk shows?

7.   What do you think is the appeal of these kinds of shows?

8.   Would you allow your children to watch talk shows?

B   Comment on this saying: "Small minds discuss people, average minds discuss events, and great minds discuss ideas."

IS TABLOID TV GETTING OUT OF HAND?

A These opinions are expressed in the article on page 103. In a group, discuss these statements. Do you agree or disagree?

1. People who watch TV talk shows are generally voyeuristic.

2. People seem to have a thirst for depravity.

3. The more lurid the topic on a talk show, the larger the audience will be.

4. Talk shows can be a good tool for education.

5. Talk shows are used to promote social good.

6. Talk shows seek out the bizarre in order to stay competitive.

7. Hostility and fights on talk shows increase ratings.

8. Talk shows are beneficial because they give information about important issues.

9. Talk shows promote open discussion about issues that would otherwise be suppressed.

10. Talk shows today fit the needs of their audiences better than television did in the past.

11. People watching a talk show don't know if they are getting the truth, and often don't care.

12. Talk shows are geared to the lowest common denominator in society.

B Read the article and answer the questions that follow.

Is Tabloid TV Getting Out of Hand?

Ted Shaw

1. The subject today is talk shows and information programming, and our first guest is Shirley Solomon, the most successful talk show host in Canadian television history. Her show, "Shirley," is syndicated in 40 markets in the United States and is seen around the world in places like Hong Kong, the Middle East, and throughout Africa. But Solomon is having doubts about the whole idea of talk shows. She sees their tendency towards voyeurism as distasteful, even though her own show engages in it every week.

2. Look at the topics for one typical week of Shirley programs last November: Should we spank our kids? Nice women who dress like tramps. I married the wrong man. Men who love boys. Shirley Solomon, 47, has taken her show where no other Canadian has gone before. But was the price too high? "My goal was to get on US television and I knew along the way I'd have to make some changes in the show," she said recently in a telephone conversation.

3. "Shirley," which is in its sixth season on CTV and is taped in Toronto, is the first successful Canadian export in a highly competitive market that now has as many as 30 talk shows in various guises and at all times of the day. But success has trapped Solomon. To compete, she and her producers have to turn the show into a circus act of freaks and curiosities. "There seems to be a thirst, not for knowledge, but for depravity," said Solomon.

4. Six years ago when she started out, she would never have considered doing programs about sexual perversities or creating confrontation in front of the cameras. Now that's the stuff of dreams on talk shows. "I'd like to take the high road on my show, but I have to tell you those shows with the more lurid topics do superbly in the ratings." What

she calls the "voyeur" tendency in talk shows began in earnest with Geraldo Rivera in the late 1980s. But Solomon figured it was a passing fad. "It isn't," she lamented. "The more you give audiences, the more they want. The more they peek through the window, the more they want to see."

5. She has done programs on employment equity, gun control, and abortion—all of them major social issues. But it's the show where a couple came on without any clothes on that got the most attention. "Television is a great tool. It can be used for the greater social good," said Solomon. "And I believe talk shows have something worthwhile to offer. But somewhere, we have lost our way."

6. She doesn't know what to do about it. As long as she has commitments to the network and stations, and if she wants to stay competitive, the "Shirley" show will have to seek out the bizarre. "I'm pushing the envelope, just like a lot of others in this business. But it's not making me happy. It really isn't."

7. A decade ago, the talk show landscape was dominated by a benign, boyish-looking Phil Donahue, who mixed discussions with celebrities and their current projects with cooking hints and the latest fashions. Then Oprah Winfrey came on the scene in 1986 and she introduced daily discussions of newsier issues. Her regional program in Chicago was expanded to become the international phenomenon it is now, seen in more than 100 countries and by an estimated audience of 15 million. Oprah opened the door, said Solomon, to a new era of talk show. "I think Oprah Winfrey personalized talk shows," she added. "She began to talk about things that had been taboo on television, partly because of her own personal experiences."

➡

8. A year or so later, Geraldo Rivera took his hard-nosed journalist's persona into the talk show arena, and all hell broke loose. The appetite for the salacious grew with Geraldo. "He lost all his credibility," said Solomon. "Remember, Geraldo is a lawyer, he's a journalist. He's not some actor-model-turned talk show host. He's the real thing. But he went right off the deep end."

9. Gradually, talk shows attracted all types as hosts, and began to appeal to a much broader audience. The lines began to be blurred between informational programming, such as "A Current Affair," and issue-oriented talk shows, like "Oprah." Curiously, "A Current Affair," which started out as a TV tabloid, has evolved into an overheated version of "Entertainment Tonight," covering mainly celebrity issues with a sheen of journalism. The stage was set by people with their own agendas, like Rush Limbaugh. His show isn't a talk show, or even a tabloid news show, but it is in-your-face reality TV. Or at least reality as seen by Limbaugh.

10. The talk show family tree has spread far and wide, and eight more talk shows were recently thrown into the hopper. The idea is to create situations where guests go after each other or the host. Surveys indicate audiences don't like it but ratings dispute that, said Solomon. "People want to see people fighting each other. They want hostility."

11. Our next guest thinks talk shows are getting a bum rap. Peter Desbarats, dean of the graduate school of journalism at the University of Western Ontario, thinks talk shows serve a worthwhile function. "The more information we are getting, the more discussion there will be," said Desbarats. "And the better it is." The alternative is more unsavory: Censorship. "When the flow of information is regulated," said Desbarats, "underground information and rumour takes its place. And that is very harmful."

12. Gossip has served a purpose in society from the earliest of times, Desbarats said. Talk shows can affect mainstream news and information programs, just like supermarket tabloids have been changing the way newspapers do business. "For a long time, television didn't fill the needs of its audience," Desbarats said. "That audience has become diversified and the more traditional forms of information aren't enough. Tabloid TV journalism has its place too, but Desbarats draws the line when these programs recreate news or dramatize it. "I have real reservations about that", he said.

13. Peter Kent is anchor of Global Television's "First News" at 6 p.m. His show comes on right before "A Current Affair" and he admits he shudders to think that a viewer will lump together his program of straight, factual news gathering and one where dramatizations are the order of the day. "The audience doesn't know if it's getting the truth, or even care," said Kent. "There is more misrepresentation of information than the public is aware of," he said.

14. For Solomon, the balance has gone out of what she does, to be replaced by cheap titillation. In the pursuit for viewers, talk shows and slick information programming aim for the lowest common denominator. "Television has always appealed to the masses and there is a whole segment of our society that until recently has been largely ignored by television."

Questions

1. Who is Shirley Solomon?

2. What is Solomon's view of talk shows?

3. What was her goal originally?

4. What does she have to do to compete with American shows?

5. How does she feel about the confrontations and perversities she shows?

6. What happened when she did programs on social issues?

7. How did talk shows change in the mid 1980s?

8. Which two people contributed to more bizarre, confrontational shows?

9. How does Peter Desbarats defend talk shows?

10. What is Peter Kent's concern about talk shows?

C Find idioms with these meanings in the paragraphs.

paragraph 1: becoming unsure of

paragraph 2: into unexplored territory

paragraph 3: in different forms

paragraph 4: do very well

paragraph 5: equal pay for equal work

paragraph 6: testing the limits

paragraph 7: began appearing

paragraph 8: someone with appropriate credentials

paragraph 9: aggressively direct

paragraph 10: attack

paragraph 11: an unfair reputation

paragraph 12: stops agreeing

paragraph 13: associate

paragraph 14: the most minimal standard

D Go back to the statements on page 102. After reading the article, have you changed any of your opinions?

 **Direct and Indirect Speech**

Direct Speech

Use direct speech to report what someone said using the speaker's exact words. Direct speech is usually used in story telling, fiction, and newspaper or magazine writing.

To show that you are using direct speech, use a comma after the introductory verb, and quotation marks on either side of the speaker's exact words. Capitalize the first word in the quote.

> Shakespeare said, "To be or not to be?"

 Punctuate the following sentences to show direct speech.

1. Neil Armstrong said one small step for man one giant step for mankind.

2. Albert Einstein said energy equals mass times the speed of light squared.

3. Ann Landers said people who drink to drown their sorrows should be told that sorrows know how to swim.

4. A well-known proverb says never put off until tomorrow what you can do today.

5. A famous bumper sticker says don't follow me I'm lost.

6. Benjamin Disraeli said the reason you have one mouth and two ears is so you can listen twice as much as you talk.

7. Confucius said to know the road ahead ask someone who is coming back.

8. Victor Hugo said no army can stop an idea whose time has come.

9. An Arabian proverb says if the camel gets its nose inside the tent its body will soon follow.

10. Al Capone once said I don't even know what street Canada is on.

Indirect Speech

Use indirect speech to report what a speaker said without using his or her exact words. Use **that** to introduce the speaker's words.

> The talk show host **said that**...

Indirect speech requires several grammatical changes.

1. **Verb changes:** Verbs in the main clause move one tense to the past.

> She said, "The singer **is** no good."
>
> She said that the singer **was** no good.
>
> He said, "The actress **can** have any role she **wants**."
>
> He said that the actress **could** have any role she **wanted**.

2. **Adverbial changes:** Adverbials become more distant in time and space.

> Someone said, "Gina doesn't want to appear in **this** movie."
>
> Someone said that Gina didn't want to appear in **that** movie.
>
> He said, "You heard the rumour **here** first".
>
> He said that he had heard the rumour **there** first.

 Change the statements into indirect speech. Make the necessary changes.

1.   We said, "We only appear on talk shows if we are well paid."

2.   Her parents said, "We don't trust you here alone all weekend."

3.   He said, "The talk show is on too late for me to watch."

4.   The gossip said, "I hear she is getting married here."

5.   The teenage boy said, "I am tired of this hairstyle."

6.   The female guest on the show said, "I believe in capital punishment."

7.   Susan said, "I have to turn on the television before 'Oprah' starts."

8.   Fred said, "I hear the next guest made his name in B movies."

9.   The guest shouted, "I think everyone here is a voyeur."

10. The security guard said, "This outburst is not acceptable."

CANADIAN CAPSULES

In a recent poll, 80 percent of Canadians surveyed said that they thought they could believe what they saw on television.

DRUG ALERT

CBC

VIDEO ACTIVITY 5

A   Work in a group to discuss these questions.

1. Would you be angry if someone in your family opened your mail?

2. Besides mail, what else do you feel you have a right to keep private?

3. Do you think teenagers should have a right to absolute privacy in their rooms?

B   Watch the video. Summarize the information by answering these questions.

1. What are the two sides of the controversy over the use of the Barringer Drug Alert System?

2. Suzanne G's daughter has been involved with drugs such as marijuana, LSD, and ecstasy. What arguments does Suzanne give in favour of the drug kit?

3. Allison H says she has used "pot" at parties but didn't like it. In what way does she think use of the kit would be counterproductive to good parent-child relations?

4. Dr. Bloudoff feels that awareness of the kit helps to raise the issue of drug use, which is positive. What does he say about the issue of trust?

5. Why does Dr. Kaufman feel the kit steers parents in the wrong direction? What does she argue for instead?

6. What rights does Dr. Kaufman think both parents and children have?

C Give your opinion of the issues raised in the video. Discuss these questions in a group.

1. Do you agree with Dr. Bloudoff's argument that if we test pilots, athletes, and truck drivers for drug use, there is no reason not to test teenagers who may be at risk? Are the situations the same?

2. Do you think that Allison and Mrs. G's daughter can be compared? What differences can you identify?

3. Do you feel that Dr. Kaufman addresses the problem of teenage drug use realistically?

4. Where do you think parents' rights stop and children's rights begin in the question of drug use?

WRITE ABOUT IT

The Right to Know

Write about one of the following topics.

a) Have TV talk shows gone too far?

or

b) How far should parents go to protect their teenagers?

PERFECT YOUR ENGLISH

Where Words Come From

Many English words have found their way into other languages. The newspapers regularly carry stories of purists trying to remove English words from other languages. It's an uphill battle because the migration of words from one language to another is as old as language itself. Indeed, English too has been tremendously enriched over the centuries by words from other languages. Let's look at some examples.

Thirty percent of English words are of French origin. Eight percent come from Latin. Japanese and Italian each account for seven percent of English vocabulary. Other contributions have come from Spanish (six percent), German and Greek (five percent), African languages, Russian, and Yiddish (four percent), Arabic, Hindi, and Chinese (two percent), and Hebrew, Indonesian, Norwegian, Portuguese, Swedish, and Vietnamese (one percent). Other contributions have come from nearly every other language on earth.

A   Work in groups. Match the "English" words listed below with the languages they come from.

1.	banjo, zombie, tote	a)	Arabic
2.	pogrom, samovar, steppe	b)	Greek
3.	goulash, hussar, paprika	c)	Japanese
4.	moccasin, papoose, toboggan	d)	Latin
5.	ketchup, kowtow, tea	e)	Yiddish
6.	rickshaw, tycoon, kimono	f)	Chinese
7.	budgie, kangaroo, boomerang	g)	Native American
8.	bazaar, shawl, caravan	h)	Persian
9.	thug, pajamas, shampoo	i)	Icelandic
10.	algebra, lemon, giraffe	j)	French
11.	schlep, nosh, klutz	k)	Hindi
12.	gesundheit, kindergarten, dunk	l)	Australian
13.	machine, chance, cigarette	m)	African
14.	geyser, rune, saga	n)	Russian
15.	phone, kudos, agnostic	o)	Hungarian
16.	data, orbit, urban	p)	German

B   1.   Add words from your language that are used in English.

   2.   Give examples of English words that are used in your language.

AT LAST

Now that you have finished the unit, go back to the activity "What's Your Take On This?" and discuss the questions again.

WHAT MOTIVATES US?

How Motivated Are You?

In a group, discuss these questions.

1. Which do you think is a bigger predictor of success: intelligence or temperament?

2. Do you know anyone you would describe as highly-motivated?

3. What characteristics do you think contribute most to a person's success in life?

4. To what extent do you think that success is influenced by luck?

5. To what extent do you think that success is influenced by hard work?

6. Can we inherit interests and character traits or do we develop them ourselves?

7. What makes a person a good communicator?

WHAT'S YOUR EMOTIONAL IQ?

A   Read the introduction to this text. Then close your book and discuss the information with your partner.

Emotional Intelligence

Daniel Goleman

Introduction

1. It was a steamy afternoon, the kind of day that makes people sullen with discomfort. I was heading home, and as I stepped onto a bus, I was startled to be greeted by the driver, a middle-aged man with an enthusiastic smile. "Hi! How're you doing?" he said. He greeted each rider in the same way. As the bus crawled through the gridlock, the driver gave a lively commentary: "…there was a terrific sale at that store, a wonderful exhibit at this museum, had we heard about the movie that just opened down the block?" By the time people got off, they had shaken off their sullen shells. When the driver called out, "So long, have a great day!" each of us gave a smiling response.

2. That memory has stayed with me for close to 20 years. I consider the bus driver a man who was truly successful at what he did. Contrast him with Jason, a straight-A student at a Florida high school who was fixated on getting into Harvard Medical School. When a physics teacher gave Jason an 80 on a quiz, the boy believed his dream was in jeopardy. He took a butcher knife to school, and in a struggle the teacher was stabbed in the collarbone. How could someone of obvious intelligence do something so irrational?

3. The answer is that high IQ does not necessarily predict who will succeed in life. Psychologists agree that IQ contributes only about 20 percent to the factors that determine success. A full 80 percent comes from other factors, including what I call emotional intelligence. The following are some of the major qualities that make up emotional intelligence and how they can be developed.

B Before you continue reading, work in a group. Decide whether these statements are **true** or **false**.

1. Understanding your emotions has a minor impact on how successfully you live your life.

2. Self-awareness is the ability to ignore your gut feelings (instincts).

3. People can learn to control their instincts if they are made aware of them.

4. Most people are able to control **when** they feel emotions such as anger.

5. Most people can control the **length of time** they feel an emotion.

6. Love is the emotion that people find the most difficult to control.

7. It is healthy to express angry feelings openly.

8. Finding an explanation for someone else's irritating behavior is counterproductive.

9. Highly successful people are generally optimistic, enthusiastic people.

10. Optimism and pessimism are less important than intelligence in achieving goals.

11. Learning to catch negative feelings and reroute them can make a person more optimistic.

12. It is not really possible for children to control their impulses if they are tempted with a reward such as candy.

13. It is possible to predict which children will become difficult adolescents.

14. Keeping long-term goals in sight is an effective way to avoid impulsive actions.

15. Reading others' emotions is important to being a good communicator.

16. People who network frequently don't achieve success because they are too busy to concentrate on their work.

C Now skim the text for the answers to the true/false questions.

Self-Awareness

4. The ability to recognize a feeling as it happens is the keystone of emotional intelligence. People with greater certainty about their emotions are better pilots of their lives. Developing self-awareness requires tuning in to the gut feelings that can occur without a person being consciously aware of them. For example, when people who fear snakes are shown a picture of a snake, sensors on their skin will detect sweat, a sign of anxiety, even though the people say they do not feel fear. The sweat shows up even when a picture is presented so rapidly that the subject has no conscious awareness of seeing it.

5. Through deliberate effort we can become more aware of our gut feelings. Take someone who is annoyed by a rude encounter for hours

➡

after it occurred. He may be oblivious to his continued irritability and surprised when someone calls attention to it. But if he stops and evaluates his feelings, he can change them.

Mood Management

6. Emotional self-awareness is the building block of the next fundamental of emotional intelligence: being able to shake off a bad mood. Bad as well as good moods spice life and build character. The key is balance. We often have little control over when we are swept by emotion. But we can have some say in how long that emotion will last. Psychologist Dianne Tice of Case Western Reserve University in Cleveland asked more than 400 men and women about their strategies for escaping foul moods. Her research, along with that of other psychologists, provides valuable information on how to change a bad mood.

7. Of all the moods that people want to escape, rage seems to be the hardest to deal with. When someone in another car cuts you off on the highway, your reflexive thought may be, "That jerk! He could have hit me! I can't let him get away with that!" The more you stew, the angrier you get. Such is the stuff of hypertension and reckless driving.

8. What should you do to relieve rage? One myth is that ventilating will make you feel better. In fact, researchers have found that expressing anger is one of the worst strategies. Outbursts of rage pump up the brain's arousal system, leaving you more angry, not less. A more effective technique is consciously reinterpreting a situation in a more positive light. In the case of the driver who cuts you off, you might tell yourself, "Maybe he had some emergency." This is one of the most potent ways, Tice found, to put anger to rest.

Self-motivation

9. Positive motivation—the marshaling of feelings of enthusiasm, zeal, and confidence—is paramount for achievement. Studies of Olympic athletes, world-class musicians, and chess grand masters show that their common trait is the ability to motivate themselves to pursue relentless training routines.

10. To motivate yourself for any achievement requires clear goals and a can-do attitude. Psychologist Martin Seligman of the University of Pennsylvania in Philadelphia advised the MetLife insurance company to hire job applicants who tested high on optimism but failed the normal aptitude test. Compared with sales people who passed the aptitude test but scored high in pessimism, this group made 21 percent more sales in their first year and 57 percent more in their second.

11. A pessimist is likely to interpret rejection as meaning, "I'm a failure; I'll never make a sale." Optimists tell themselves, "I'm using the wrong approach" or "That customer was in a bad mood." By blaming failure on the situation, not themselves, optimists are motivated to make that next call.

12. A predisposition to a positive or negative outlook may be inborn, but with effort and practice, pessimists can learn to think more hopefully. Psychologists have documented that if you can catch negative, self-defeating thoughts as they occur, you can reframe the situation in less catastrophic term.

Impulse Control

13. The essence of emotional self-regulation is the ability to delay impulse in the service of a goal. The importance of this trait to success was shown in an experiment begun in the 1960s by psychologist Walter Mischel at a preschool on the Stanford University campus in California. Children were told they could have a single treat, such as a marshmallow, right now. However, if they'd wait while the experimenter ran an errand, they could have two marshmallows. Some preschoolers grabbed the marshmallow immediately, but others were able to wait. To sustain themselves in their struggle, they covered their eyes so they wouldn't see the temptation, talked to themselves, and even tried to sleep.

14. The interesting part of this experiment came in the follow-up. The children who as four-year-olds had been able to wait for the two marshmallows were, as adolescents, still able to delay gratification in pursuing their goals. They were more socially competent and self-assertive, and better able to cope with life's frustrations. In contrast, the kids who grabbed the one marshmallow were, as adolescents, more likely to be stubborn, indecisive, and stressed.

15. The ability to resist impulse can be developed with practice. When you're faced with an immediate temptation, think of your long-term goals—whether they be losing weight or getting a medical degree. You'll then find it easier to keep from settling for the single marshmallow.

People Skills

16. The capacity to know how another feels is important on the job, in romance and friendship, and in the family. We transmit and catch moods from one another on a subtle, almost imperceptible level. The way someone says thank you, for instance, can leave us feeling dismissed, patronized, or genuinely appreciated. The more adroit we are at discerning the feelings behind other people's signals, the better we control the signals we send.

17. The importance of good interpersonal skills was demonstrated by psychologists Robert Kelley and Janet Caplan at Bell Labs in Naperville, Ill. The labs are staffed by engineers and scientists who are all at the apex of academic IQ tests. Some of those studied emerged as stars, while others languished.

18. What accounted for the difference? The standout performers had a network with a wide range of people. "When a non-star encountered a technical problem," Kelley observed, "he called various technical gurus and then waited, wasting time while his calls went unreturned. Star performers rarely faced such situations because they build reliable networks before they needed them. So when the stars called someone, they almost always got a faster answer." No matter what their IQ, once again it was emotional intelligence that separated the stars from the average performers.

GETTING THE MOST OUT OF YOURSELF

Work in a group and discuss these questions.

1. Have you ever had a bad habit that you were able to overcome?

2. Do you feel you are a highly-motivated personality type or a laid-back personality type?

3. What are some of the things that make you really angry?

4. What do you do when you are angry that helps you cool down?

5. Are there any points in the article you have just read that are of particular relevance to you or to anyone you know?

6. What do you think are your most positive qualities?

GRAMMAR FOCUS — Questions

WH-Information Questions

WH-information questions request a response that includes some specific type of information.

In addition to simple questions that ask **when**, **where**, **who**, **why**, **how** and **what**, there are question phrases that ask for more specific information.

> **What** + noun (**time**, **kind**, **size**, **colour**, etc.)
>
> **Which** + noun (offers a choice)
>
> **How much** + noun
>
> **How many** + noun
>
> **How** + adverb (**often**, **soon**, **slowly**, etc.)
>
> **How** + adjective (**tall**, **big**, **smart**, **far**, etc.)
>
> **How long** (for time)
>
> **How old** (for age)

 A Write ten questions to ask a partner using some of the forms shown above. Then work with a partner to ask and answer your questions.

B Write ten questions about the information in the article "Emotional Intelligence" using some of the forms shown in the box above.

Negative Questions

Questions are generally asked in the affirmative. Negative questions are often used to express a sense of surprise.

> Can't you speak Russian? (I thought you could.)

Negative questions anticipate a particular response which is usually negative.

> Can't you speak Russian?   No, I can't.

CANADIAN CAPSULES

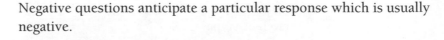
"Every life is a work of art, shaped by the person who lives it."

Anonymous

Match the questions to the answers.

1. Wasn't that surprising news?

2. Haven't they heard that joke before?

3. Won't the weather affect their plans?

4. Didn't you meet before?

5. Can't we just return it if it doesn't work?

6. Wasn't that John on the phone?

7. Shouldn't somebody tell him to stop talking?

8. Can't you use a computer?

9. Haven't you ever been to New York?

10. Aren't we a little early?

---

a) Only if you have the sales slip.

b) I don't think so. They all have umbrellas.

c) No. I'm a techno-nerd.

d) I don't really like big cities.

e) Not me. He's my boss.

f) No, it wasn't. It was Alice.

g) I don't think so. The invitation said 8:00.

h) Most people already knew about it.

i) I don't think so. They seem to be laughing.

j) No. We've never met.

DOING WHAT YOU LOVE

CBC ◉   LISTENING ACTIVITY **5**   *Interview with Barbara Sher,*
Career Counsellor

A   Work in a group to discuss these questions.

1. How many people do you know who are happy in their jobs?

2. Why do you think most people choose the jobs they do?

3. If you could make a living doing something you love to do, what would it be?

4. What would you need to do to pursue your dream?

B   Listen to the interview. Then summarize the ideas by answering these questions with a partner.

1. What are two reasons people are unhappy in their jobs?

2. What is the meaning of Benjamin Disraeli's saying "Most people will go to their graves with their music still in them."?

3. What does the example about the horticulturist say about most people?

4. How does Barbara Sher find out what people are gifted at?

5. Summarize the story of the woman who loved gorillas.

6. What does Barbara say about finding out what you love and how to do it?

7. What does she say about making a living?

8. What idea did Barbara give the cab driver?

9. Why does Barbara do what she does?

C After you listen, discuss these questions in a group.

1. What special skills and abilities do you have?

2. What do you "love" to do?

3. How could you pursue your dreams?

WRITE ABOUT IT

Pursuing a Dream

Write about your dreams, and how you could pursue them.

PERFECT YOUR ENGLISH

Colourful Language

Many expressions we use in English make reference to colour. An angry person may be described as "red in the face." A person who is sad or depressed may be "feeling blue." Interestingly, however, only three colours in English can be used as verbs: "redden," "whiten," and "blacken."

Try the quiz below to see what you know about colours and their connotations.

1. The colour green is used to describe:
   a) envy
   b) happiness
   c) fear

2. A "red-letter day" is one of:
   a) traumatic events
   b) good fortune
   c) bad fortune

3. "True blue" means
   a) sincere
   b) intelligent
   c) loyal

4. To "paint the town red" means to:
   a) wake up early
   b) have a wild time
   c) go sightseeing in town

5. In North America, white is a symbol of:

    a) purity

    b) fear

    c) illness

6. Something "out of the blue" means:

    a) something unexpected

    b) something that brings happiness

    c) something that brings sadness

7. To be "red faced" means:

    a) to be excited

    b) to be embarrassed

    c) to be worried

8. To "black out" means to:

    a) become very angry

    b) become very sick

    c) lose consciousness

9. "Once in a blue moon" means:

    a) often

    b) sometimes

    c) rarely

10. If you have a "green thumb," you are:

    a) a good baker

    b) a good gardener

    c) a good musician

11. Bright yellow is associated with:

    a) anger

    b) intelligence

    c) excitement

12. The "blues" are:

    a) a kind of music

    b) a kind of poetry

    c) a style of painting

13. Where does a "white-collar worker" work?

    a) in a factory

    b) in a mine

    c) in an office

14. If you have a "yellow streak," you are:

    a) angry

    b) brave

    c) cowardly

15. To "put out the red carpet" means to:

    a) treat someone well

    b) be rude to someone

    c) be angry with someone

16. A "greenhorn" is:

    a) inexperienced

    b) excited

    c) embarrassed

17. The "black sheep" of the family is:

    a) evil

    b) different

    c) in disgrace

18. A "red eye" is:

    a) an eye disease

    b) an overnight airplane flight

    c) an angry person

19. The "black market" is a place to buy something:

    a) cheaply

    b) quickly

    c) illegally

20. The term "shrinking violet" is used to describe someone who is:

    a) shy

    b) thin

    c) sad

AT LAST

Now that you have finished the unit, go back to the activity "What's Your Take On This?" and discuss the questions again.

Topics for Debate

Topic: The global spread of the Internet is a positive development.

Pro

– It promotes exchange of information.

– It democratizes access to information.

– It reduces communication time.

–

–

–

Con

– It creates "haves" and "have nots."

– It gives America hegemony.

– It is impossible to control content.

–

–

–

Topic: People would never immigrate to Canada if they could get into the United States.

Pro

– The United States offers greater economic opportunity.

– The climate is better in the United States.

– The United States is better known.

–

–

–

Con

– There is less crime in Canada.

– There is more respect for cultural diversity in Canada.

– Medicare is universal in Canada.

–

–

–

Topic: Participation in competitive sports is beneficial.

Pro

– It develops self-discipline.

– It promotes good physical conditioning.

– It develops self-confidence.

– It teaches the value of hard work.

–

–

–

Con

– It makes people aggressive.

– Winning becomes more important than playing the game.

– It takes time away from intellectual activities.

– It leads to excesses and physical injuries.

–

–

–

Topic: The best way to prevent crime is to get tougher with criminals.

Pro

– Criminals have little to lose if they are caught.

– Stronger sentences would be a deterrent.

– The public has no respect for the courts.

– Crime is increasing under the current system.

–

–

–

Con

– There is no proof that stronger sentences reduce crime.

– Prisons are not effective, as most criminals re-offend.

– It is better to address the social causes of crime.

– Treatment, not punishment, will deter crime.

–

–

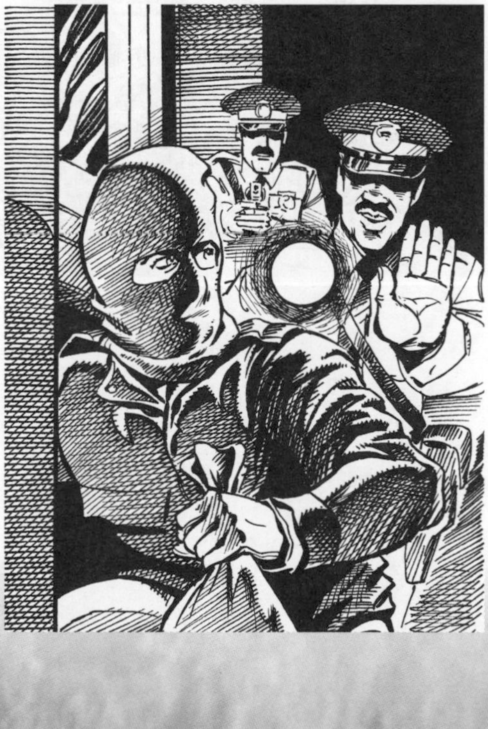

Topic: The government should ban tobacco advertising.

Pro

– Tobacco is a dangerous product.

– Teenagers are very susceptible to suggestion.

– Cigarette ads are misleading.

–

–

–

Con

– Ads have little effect on influencing people to start smoking.

– People will smoke regardless of advertising.

– Tobacco companies finance sports and cultural events.

–

–

–

Topic: Medical research should get money any way it can.

Pro

– Government revenues are not limitless.

– Many important advances would not have occurred without private fundraising.

– Taxes would have to be raised to generate the money.

–

–

–

Con

– Medical research has an impact on all of us, so funding should be a government concern.

– Private fundraising campaigns can't generate enough money.

– Company contributions raise conflict of interest issues.

–

–

–

Topic: People who cause accidents should be held responsible.

Pro

– Drunk drivers knowingly take risks and endanger others.

– The possibility of penalties would make people think twice.

– Landlords who don't make repairs contribute to accidents.

– Substance abuse is a choice that endangers others.

–

–

–

Con

– It's not always possible to know who is responsible.

– Not all accidents are caused by irresponsible behaviour.

– You risk being unfair to innocent people.

– Sometimes two people are equally responsible for an accident.

–

–

–

Topic: Genetic research should be discontinued.

Pro

– Genetic research is tampering with nature.

– It is open to abuse by insurance companies.

– Employers can abuse the information they get.

– It can lead to unethical experiments.

–

–

–

Con

– It offers the hope of cures for terrible illnesses.

– You can't hold back the march of progress.

– It would be immoral not to find more cures.

– Research can be regulated so that it isn't used inappropriately.

–

–

–

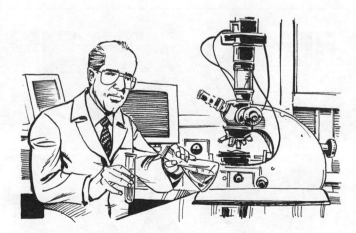

Topic: Tabloid TV is polluting the public airwaves.

Pro

– It is increasingly seedy and lurid.

– It blurs the lines between fantasy and reality.

– Some topics should not be aired in public.

– It gives a false impression of our cultural values.

–

–

–

Con

– Viewers can distinguish between fiction and reality.

– If it's so popular it must have something to offer.

– It's healthy to discuss things that are facts of life.

– People aren't forced to watch; they can always switch off or turn to PBS.

–

–

–

Topic: The self-improvement movement is laudable.

Pro

– If you don't help yourself, no one else will.

– There is always room for improvement in everything we do.

– Progress comes from the will to do better.

– There is nothing wrong with wanting the best for yourself.

–

–

–

Con

– People waste time and effort on things they can't change.

– People should make more effort to be content with what they have.

– Many self-improvement schemes are scams.

– Happiness doesn't come from always striving for more.

–

–

–

Appendix: Irregular Verbs

Many past participles are the same as the regular or irregular past tense forms. Irregular past participles are shown in bold type below.

Present	Past	Past participle
arise	arose	**arisen**
awake	awoke	**awaken**
be	was, were	**been**
beat	beat	**beaten**
become	became	**become**
begin	began	**begun**
bite	bit	**bitten**
bleed	bled	bled
blow	blew	**blown**
break	broke	**broken**
bring	brought	brought
build	built	built
buy	bought	bought
catch	caught	caught
choose	chose	**chosen**
come	came	**come**
cost	cost	cost
cut	cut	cut
dig	dug	dug
do	did	**done**
draw	drew	**drawn**
drink	drank	**drunk**
drive	drove	**driven**
eat	ate	**eaten**
fall	fell	**fallen**
feed	fed	fed
feel	felt	felt
find	found	found
fly	flew	**flown**
forbid	forbade	**forbidden**
forget	forgot	**forgotten**
forgive	forgave	**forgiven**
freeze	froze	**frozen**
get	got	**gotten** (got)
give	gave	**given**
go	went	**gone**
grow	grew	**grown**
have	had	had
hear	heard	heard
hide	hid	**hidden**
hit	hit	hit

Present	Past	Past participle
hold	held	held
hurt	hurt	hurt
keep	kept	kept
know	knew	**known**
lay	laid	laid
lead	led	led
leave	left	left
let	let	let
lie	lay	**lain**
lose	lost	lost
make	made	made
mean	meant	meant
meet	met	met
pay	paid	paid
put	put	put
read	read	read
ride	rode	**ridden**
ring	rang	**rung**
rise	rose	**risen**
run	ran	**ran**
see	saw	**seen**
sell	sold	sold
send	sent	sent
shake	shook	**shaken**
shine	shone	shone
shoot	shot	shot
show	showed	shown
shrink	shrank	**shrunk**
shut	shut	shut
sing	sang	**sung**
sit	sat	sat
sleep	slept	slept
speak	spoke	**spoken**
spread	spread	spread
spring	sprang	**sprung**
stand	stood	stood
steal	stole	**stolen**
stink	stank	**stunk**
swear	swore	**sworn**
swim	swam	**swum**
take	took	taken
teach	taught	taught
tear	tore	**torn**
tell	told	told
think	thought	thought
throw	threw	**thrown**
understand	understood	understood
wake	woke	**woken**
wear	wore	**worn**
win	won	won
write	wrote	**written**

هذا الكتاب مهم، شيِّق

如果你读了过本书 你会感到"绝了", 太棒了! 让人难以忘记。

ESTE LIBRO ES MUY INTERESANTE ! BUENA SUERTE !!!

英語は易しい.
この本は面白い
さようなら.

Ce livre est très intéressant !

ㅡㅁㅁㅎ ㅎㅎㅁㅎㅁ ㅡ Cãmmãm
excellent pour apprendre !

BONJOUR

Böngna Jaunniõ

TSARA ITY BOKY ITY . VELOMA

Ce n'est qu'un début ...

Este livro é muito interessante

HAS ARRIVAT FINS ACÍ, MOLT BÉ NANO !